Don't Shake the Spoon
A Journal of Prison Writing

Volume 2

WWW.EXCHANGE-FOR-CHANGE.ORG

Don't Shake the Spoon
A Journal of Prison Writing
Volume 2
Copyright © 2019 Exchange for Change

Editor: Enzu Castellanos
Co-Editors: Kathie Klarreich, Nick Vagnoni
Editorial Intern: Evan Balikos
Production Volunteers: Clayre Benzadon, Khadijah Brown
Cover Design: Tom Beeckman
Cover Photo: Courtesy of WFOR- TV/CBS4
Publisher: Exchange for Change, Kathie Klarreich, Director

WWW.EXCHANGE-FOR-CHANGE.ORG

2103 Coral Way, 2nd Floor
Miami, FL 33145
(305) 771-3241

Excerpt from "Don't Shake the Spoon"
by Eduardo Martinez*

We starve for more than just nutrition. We hunger for attention, forgiveness, respect, redemption. These pages are the D.O.C.'s dirty dishes: raw, uncut, no rocks, no filter. Meals of sadness and sunrays, sugar-watered tears and salty, force-fed fears. We offer you everything we have. Everything you deserve.
Eat society's delicacies, as the stereotypical tune is drowned by the bass of our hearts. Eat our words, digest our stories. Eat 'til you're disgusted, 'til awareness replaces your appetite. Fill your conscience with everything . . . everything but broken promises.
EAT! EAT! EAT!
Then feed us changes, but please . . .
Don't Shake the Spoon . . .

*This piece is published in its entirety in DSTS Volume 1.

Introduction

Exchange for Change strives to bring more writing opportunities to our students in correctional facilities, and to bring their voices to the outside community. That's why this journal exists. Three years ago, a group of E4C instructors sought a way to bring our students' writing to all the places our writers can't go–into libraries and cafes, book fairs and public readings, and community conversations about mass incarceration. We bound their writing together and placed it in the hands of students, community members, politicians and local leaders, friends and supporters, and, most importantly, the families waiting at home for their loved ones.

This second volume continues to showcase the work of students participating in varied curricula that cover fiction, creative nonfiction, poetry, and everything in-between, from songwriting to Shakespeare to writing in Spanish.

Prison literature, or writings from prisons, from Paul's "Letters to Corinthians" to MLK Jr.'s "Letter from Birmingham Jail," whether intimate or public-facing, are often calls to social action. Accordingly, some of the works in this volume reflect, illuminate, or explore, and at times, foment social action.

To set the tone for these explorations, we asked writers to consider the idea of "now." Contributors obliquely peruse and explicitly dissect that idea in ways you might expect, but also in ways unexpected and lyrical, honest and self-aware, tender, but not soft. Overall, the work in this volume represents what happens when previously silenced voices are heard, challenged, and nurtured.

Table of Contents

He'd Rather
by Jonathan Arce

He'd rather draw on colored paper instead
       of the metal table.
He'd rather sing in the morning instead
       of at noon after lunch.
He'd rather speak to a friend instead of to himself.
He'd rather keep his nob instead of losing it.
He'd rather write letters during the morning hours instead
of at night, when the cell is
       dim and the cell block is loud.

He'd rather count the sets and reps of a thousand push-ups
instead of the bricks inside
       his locked cell.

He'd rather glance at a newscaster
       instead of at a Sheriff's Deputy.
He'd rather everyone speak of him as a high school grad
instead of as a murderer, at
       age fourteen, with a high-profile case.

He'd rather be in the comfort of his home instead of in a
       locked cell that he views as
          home until who knows how long.

Packed Bags
by Emilio C. Fernandez

    Mom's a time traveler. Goes to the past whenever she wants to remember why she has a grudge on you. "I forgive, but I don't forget," she says. Lately, she journeys to the future, one where her son is free to come home, eat her tilapia ceviche and caramel flan, trying to change the present, somehow wake up from this nightmare of being a prison mom.

    Sons are supposed to visit their mothers on the weekend, not the other way around. These visits are tougher on her than on me. I get closer to the exit. She actually has to come inside, then eventually leave me here again.

    Drives out to nowhere tucked inside a swamp, parks her Ford Ranger, glimpses the inescapable razor wire fortress, a thousand tiny mirrors show her reflection. Brought her bags again. They look fuller. Not the ones branded Fendi or Louis Vitton. No, these are filled with hurt and regret, sleepless nights under dark brown eyes. Doesn't like wearing socks, but does here. Says this is the last place she wants to be barefoot. After waiting what seems like hours, they put her in the room. They don't ask her to squat and cough, but having some woman grope and probe your intimate parts is no consolation prize.

    In this moment of violation, she wonders where she went wrong raising the oldest of two children. How could she have parented differently? She blames herself. Obviously can't blame me, I'm still her little angel. I see it clearly through held back tears, the way she looks at me, her longing touch.

    Knowing we can't go back, she yearns to go forward, but we're stuck in the clutches of the present. One foot must remain firmly planted in the reality of the moment or she will unravel like a worn-out piece of clothing as this incarceration pulls on the thread of her emotional stability. I can see this all plainly painted on her face, real as her make-up. Covers it up well, but I'm a master of masks. Peek-a-boo. I see you. Doesn't know that of course, but don't tell her. Needs to be strong for me, my rock, my source of strength.

Visits reduced to a masquerade ball, all curtsies and bows, full of formalities, devoid of all substance. That's when I want to time travel, go to the past where I can break my arm and say, "Mom, this hurts!"

She can look me straight in teary, hazel eyes saying, "Everything's going to be all right son."

That's impossible now. Too much uncertainty. Doesn't know what to believe. 2030, so far away. Will her health last? What about her sanity? Every sliver of hope is a termite-eaten rung on a wooden ladder.

We are both prisoners. One with concrete walls, the other within the confines of her skull. She built it, I threw her in. I have the key, yet I'm too scared to let her out. Terrified of so many walled up emotions. Afraid of all the tears to be shed. For now, she relies on her time travel; whether to a grudge-filled past or a fragile future built on mere possibilities, anything is better than a present full of prison.

The Unexpected
by Summer Reign Heath

The Unexpected. Conscious of the unconscious but still conscious of nothing.

You hate me…Why?

Is it because my words are lethal? Lethal like Bruce Lee right before he took his last fall? Hurt from the touch of society's standards, but that's ok enjoy it while it lasts. Because in my mind I'm going to get the last laugh. I'm vicious like a lioness who is hunting her bleeding prey. A lioness who has been set apart by her pride. Not wanted, pushed out, but still I stand proud. Listen, you inhale the same air I breathe. I'm stronger than you think so my mind you cannot deceive. Awoken to defeat as numerous times before. Got up, dusted off. I am a lioness, hear me roar! Loyal since birth but trouble stays following me. I'll die to get my point across, you will never defeat me. Feel my pain, while insanity takes control of my brain. The professionals say: He'll be ok. He can maintain. Maintain in a society so full of hate. I've fallen weak and tried to take my own life to escape my mistake. Now that was unexpected.

Unexpected is what is not known, but what is known is expected. How can society put up standards for what it doesn't understand? To be part of something you need a set of rules. I'm good! People have fought long and hard to be a part of a society of acceptance. But why? Just be yourselves. When you are scared of what people think, you will always be just another one of society's puppets. But to be free, to be alive in life is to be honest with yourself. Now I don't push my way of life on no one; you either know me or you don't. This is my first time writing a piece about the pride. I am a lioness like it or not, who stands proud and tall, ready to face life's situations at a moment's call. Was I called for this or just blessed? This I don't know, but I will conquer this unexpected quest! Welcome to my jungle.

ARE YOU KIDDING?!: A Lifer's View of the Death Penalty
by James Doyle

Some time ago, I sat alone in my prison cell reading a Christian magazine. One article in particular caught my eye. It was entitled, "Rethinking the Death Penalty." In it, the author laid out his polemic against the death penalty. Nothing new; he presented the same vague generalities and shallow understanding of the issue I have heard for years. However, he made one statement that really shocked me. Arguing that the death penalty is not necessary for public safety, he asserted, "With modern advancements in the corrections industry, developed nations are fully capable of keeping criminals locked away for life." (The Banner. February 2016. 21). I have only one question: ARE YOU KIDDING?!

Everyone seems to have their own opinion on the death penalty: politicians, professionals, the public. Some clamor for execution; others decry it as inhumane. Now they all have the right to hold their opinions as well as the freedom to express them, however, they all have one thing in common: None of them has spent significant time inside a prison. Rather, their opinions are based on media sensationalism, industry propaganda, and personal agendas. Personal experience is conspicuously absent from the conversation. As a man with a life sentence, presently in the midst of my fourth decade behind the fences, I represent the voice of personal experience. And I say keeping criminals locked away for life is inhumane. The death penalty is truly the humane option.

On April 25, 1985, I pled guilty to first degree murder in exchange for a life sentence. Like the rest of the misinformed, I felt it was more humane than the death penalty. Two days later, the Florida Department of Corrections (DOC) welcomed me to my new home. It traumatized me with the two-month hazing it calls the reception process. Then the DOC transferred me to Union Correctional Institution in Raiford. I was in shock but I was not abandoned. Whenever I was lonely and needed the comfort of a friendly voice, I could call my family. Someone was always there for me. Sadly, this would not last.

The first to fall away was Nanny. It may have been July 1985. Still new in prison, I lived in a constant state of anxiety, confusion and fear. Early one evening, I went to the little patch of grass in front of Dorm 57, where two blue phones hung on the slime green wall. I picked up one of the black receivers and pressed the little silver buttons, entering Nanny's number. "Hello." The operator informed Nanny she had a collect call from James Doyle. "Will you accept the charges?" In a voice filled with desperation, Nanny replied, "Nooo," and hung up. I did not understand.

Others soon followed suit. I sent Amy a wedding gift: she did not acknowledge it. I sent everyone Christmas cards: only my parents and my sister Diane reciprocated. Trapped between the majority of the family and Dad and me, Diane made excuses for everyone. "Everyone's fine. Busy working." But that did not make sense. I still did not understand.

I finally learned the truth through "family leaks" and Dad. In building their case against me, the State Attorney had called my family in for depositions. But first… he gave all of them a copy of my confession. I finally understood: I had committed an unpardonable sin. With the exception of Mom, Dad, and Diane, my family had turned away from me.

Eventually, I lost Mom. Though she lived in Georgia, we maintained a healthy communication. We exchanged letters and holiday cards. We talked on the phone at least once a month. She even came to visit in 1987. Then things began to change. She divorced her third husband; Garlock, the company for which she worked, went out of business; she suffered a severe concussion in an auto accident. Finally, she moved back to Rochester, New York, to be with her family. Suddenly, her letters arrived more sporadically. And then, the Phone Games.

The Phone Games began around 2005. One sunny afternoon at Zephyrhills Correctional Institution, I walked to the D-Dorm day room. Picking up the black receiver of the blue phone on the wall, I pressed the little silver buttons, entering Mom's number. "Hello." By this time, the phone system was automated. The computer put me on hold while it gave Mom instructions on how to accept my call. About a minute later, the curt voice of the computer kicked in. "Your call was not accepted. Please try again later." A few weeks later, I called Mom again. She accepted my call this time. Beginning our conversation, she asserted, "I heard you called a few weeks ago, but I was not here." Knowing she lived alone, I guessed, "I must have heard your answering machine." Caught off guard she blurted, "I don't have an answering machine." My mind went blank. I did not understand, but I was afraid to press farther.

As a dutiful son, I continued to go to that blue phone and enter her number every month. I never expected an answer, though. She almost never accepted my calls now. She was just smarter about it, waiting to hear a computer voice warn her of a call from her son before she said, "Hello." This continued until she died, May 3, 2007.

Then, I lost my dad. Though we had a tumultuous relationship in my youth because of his verbal abuse, Dad had become my best friend. He was there for me from the very beginning. Not a religious man himself, he sent me religious books he thought would be helpful and he visited me twice a week while I was in county jail. And even though he was 71 when I was arrested, he continued to visit me faithfully, regardless of where the DOC sent me. Whether I was 300 miles away at Raiford or 45 miles away at Bowling Green, I survived knowing that Dad would visit every other week. Only two things stopped him: when I was involved in a weekend chapel activity or he was incapacitated in the hospital.

Time is merciless. It has neither empathy for the elderly nor sympathy for the suffering. Over the years, I watched as the arthritis in his back and neck stooped his shoulders. The cartilage in his knees wore away; he digressed from walking independently to hobbling on a cane to supporting himself with a walker. He lived alone in this condition. With a daughter busy with her own family and a son in prison, his only help came from a dope addict who had worked with him in a print shop years before.

On June 30, 2007, Dad visited me for the last time. He seemed to have a little cold, but he left with his customary parting: "I love you and miss you, and I'll see you in two weeks." The following week, his cold made it hard for him to breathe. The dope addict got him to the hospital, where they discovered he really had pneumonia. They admitted him and put him on heavy antibiotics. His pneumonia cleared up, but he had become so weak they sent him to a convalescent center to rebuild his strength. He finally returned home on August 18; however, things were still not right. I called him on August 19. Diane was with him. She let me know that Dad had had a "bad night" and that she was going to call hospice the next day. She let me talk to him for just a moment. He ended with his customary parting: "I love you and miss you, and I'll see you in Heaven." Hospice admitted Dad on August 20. Then, on August 29, 2007, Chaplain Fortner called me into his Hardee C.I. office. Dad was gone. He was 93.

Finally, I lost Diane. The last member of my family to maintain contact with me, she grew more distant after Dad's death. She had promised Dad that she would visit me faithfully when he was gone. I held on to the hope of seeing her for five years before I was finally able to accept the truth. She would never come. She and her husband moved twice, but they never gave me their new phone number. She stopped sending me a little money for birthdays and Christmas. She sent no notes or family news, just holiday cards that simply said, "Love, Diane."

Over the years, I tried to woo her into a deeper correspondence. To her credit, she did write me two real letters. She actually vented some of her feelings as well as dismissed any possibility that I will ever be paroled. I count them as special treasures; she finally told me how she felt. Years went by until I was again called into the chaplain's office. My sister died on May 4, 2019, after a long struggle with an unspecified illness. She was 81. The last thread connecting me to my family has been severed.

Centuries ago, there was a king of a small, declining nation. It had been a great nation at one time, but now it was a vassal state to a powerful empire. Perhaps he had hopes of restoring his little nation to its former glory. Whatever the reason, he rebelled against his sovereign. Incensed, the sovereign sent his army to destroy this rebel nation. The little king fled, but he could not escape. He, along with his whole family, was dragged before the sovereign to stand judgement. The sovereign forced him to watch as soldiers murdered his seven sons. It was the last thing he ever saw. His captors gouged out his eyes and carried him away as a prisoner to their own country. There he died, the memories of failure and loss echoing through his empty heart.

A life sentence is a lot like that, with one exception. The little king lost everything immediately; I have lost everything progressively. I have dealt with the confusion of being rejected by family, the desperation of relationships growing cold, and the self-condemnation of being helpless when my parents and sister needed me. Today, the memories of failure and loss echo through my empty heart. Yes, I have a life sentence. Yet, if nothing changes, my end will be no different than it would have been if I had a death sentence: I will die in prison. But I will be forced to hear these echoes for another thirty years before I reach the place where I will hear them no longer. The death penalty is truly the humane option.

Secrets Sat Upon
by Claire Hanson

Silent waitstaff clear the detritus of our meal, unnoticed. My eyes are riveted upon Sarah as she fingers the rim of her wine glass, half-shadowed and mysterious as the setting sun danced upon the waters of the Bay. Stray light caught her ruby pendant, reminding me of our previous date.

Splendid though tonight has been, she seems preoccupied. A thoughtful frown lends a sense of gravity to her girl-next-door features. How could this bring a pang to my heart? True, this is our third date, but we have known each other for almost a year through work. Surely that makes up for the brevity of our courtship?

Were I a poet, I would write a sonnet on her dichotomous, reserved yet one-of-the-guys spirit. Were I eloquent, I would pen a haiku extolling her deliberation of word and action. Were I an artist, I would capture upon canvas her earthly divinity poised atop a clamshell.

Oh! Her emerald gaze pins me with its intensity. She sips from her wineglass–is her hand trembling?–and gently clears her throat. All else is forgotten as her dusky voice caresses me, evoking sensations of silk and smoke.

"I...I'm not sure how to tell you, but I have a secret."

"You can tell me anything," I say, curious.

She hesitates, then "I don't want to lose you."

I chuckle and take her hands. "I'm right here," I say, "no matter what."

Her gaze locks onto mine, contemplating, peering into my mind. "I haven't always been this way," she whispers.

Political Poem
by Ramon "Seattle" Grayson

The pen glides across the parchment of paper–guided, Foundations
are being set on the strengths of the people. In support of the inner-
thoughts of what should be done for them and the future of their
colonies and
families.

I would think most of the thoughts were right for those on the land at
the time, seeing those were written before slavery and taking over a
nation already belonging to another people.

Yet the pen didn't know the story it told, or how it would mold
the future, or Indian, White, African, and Asian how it would
influence what would be a nation.

The pen didn't know who was righteous and just or who was self-
righteous and unjust, it just does what it's told guided by the
intentions of the beholder.

Even over the hundreds of years, longer than a person's life, the
pen remains guided over the parchments, making decrees, policies,
laws, treaties, declaring war, tearing down what another politician
has done "for the people" doing it why just because that new
politician won?

The pen was guided by the hand, it revealed the forefathers' plan,
showing the thoughts of establishing a new life, but as years go by
the pen is used more for the guide than the people. The pen is used
because a word like equal can't be erased. The pen is guided to
create a self-righteous fate not caring of chaos or even debate with
the signing of their names they changed the original fate of what the

creator created, they want to keep on writing even when there is no space.

What Is Poverty?
by Emmett T. Cox

It's not just growing up poor, hungry. As a child we never understand what the word poverty is, so I asked my Mama, what is poverty? Mother looked at me with tears welled up in the corner of her eyes and said to me, my Son, listen to me. Listen without pity. Because, I cannot use pity. But, listen with understanding.

Mama said, Son, poverty is living in a smell that never leaves. It's a smell of young children who've ran, played all day in the sun and cannot bathe at night. It's the smell of milk that has gone sour because the refrigerator don't work 'cause there is no power. It's the smell of rotting garbage that has piled up in the alley.

Son, poverty is being tired, Mama says she always been tired. They told her at the hospital when my baby sister was born that she had chronic anemia and that she needed a corrective operation. Mama listened politely, the poor is always polite, they don't tell their business and say I don't have the money to buy the iron medication, or better, say they can't even afford to buy food for the family.

Mama said, Son, poverty is dirt. She went on to explain about the keep of her house with no money. She said every night she would wash every stitch of our school clothes, and hope they would be dry by in the morning. The dishes was washed in cold winter with no soap. Even the cheapest soap had to be saved for my sister diapers. I asked: Mama, why not hot water? She says hot water is a luxury, my Son. I. Do. Not. Have. Luxuries.

Mama said, poverty is looking for help. Do you know how it feels, when you're looking for the office of your appointment, after circling the block four or five times, then you go into this building, everyone seems to be so busy, then finally someone asks you do you need help, and they direct you to another person? After spilling all your of life to the person you're directed to speak to, you find this isn't the right office after all.

Mama said, Son, poverty is looking into a bleak future, neighbor children wouldn't even play with you, Son, I watched the bitterness in your eyes as you grew older, and started to hang out with guys in the same poverty class, I watched ya'll steal to get what you wanted, as for your baby sister, I thought life at best for her was going to be a life like mines.

The people threaten to put me in jail 'cause I couldn't afford to put ya'll in school, yes there are such things as school, but because ya'll didn't have books, pencils, crayons or paper, most of all ya'll was not in good health, due to your suffering from hunger, malnutrition.

Mama said, Son, last but not least I'm going to give you my final segment on poverty, poverty is cooking without food, cleaning without soap. Poverty is an acid that drips on pride until pride is worn away. Son, you may say that you would do something different in my situation and maybe you would in today's world. But for year, after year, after year. You, my son, will always have that smell of poverty, because you lived it, dreamed it, and ate of it.

3.850 AKA Ineffective Assistance of Counsel
by Pablo Sandoval

"Don't show them any emotion."

That's the advice I had been getting from my 'one step above a public defender' attorney for the previous four days.

Don't react when someone gets on the stand and lies on you.

Don't show hurt when the State parades the only two friends you have left and your mother as key character witnesses to try and establish that at 19 years old you were a puppet master that could teach Trump a thing or two.

Don't look at the victims' family and show any kind of remorse. And NO!!! you damn sure can't write a letter, even if you're only asking that one day they find some peace, even if it comes from believing all the lies that they're told about you.

Don't show outrage at how your co-defendant's parents are trying to still console a mother even after your jury said that it was their son that pulled the trigger.

Don't flinch when you get a mandatory four-lettered sentence (LIFE) that just seems to run on, for a shooting someone else will be getting 15 years for.

No... don't show anything.

Just stand there like your face is made out of the same stuff as the handcuffs that have been testing your wrists for the past hundred or so hours.

Be indifferent to your life being thrown away like a Styrofoam cup, unable to even be recycled.

Ok... now that we got past that let's prepare for the easy part.

Don't show anger when you're disrespected because of your blue suit or when you realize that the rules are only there to empower descendants of Willie Lynch.

Don't flinch when kids as old as your oldest daughter spit, slap, and suppress men that have been around since the fight for Civil Rights.

Don't despair when the appeals court upholds a future for you with less substance than a handful of air or when you cut off the few people that have come back into your life because your time hurts them too much.

That wasn't too hard, was it?

Now let's forget that you've received more good advice from crooks that never picked up books.

Let's forget that one of your happiest moments was when you realized that your daughter lied to you when at nine years old she told you in all seriousness, "Daddy, I've decided that I can only wait for you till I'm thirteen, OK?"

Let's forget that the last time you held her as a free man was... well... never.

Let's forget that you've forgotten what freedom even is.

All because you forgot to feel.

Basketball Game: 50 and Over
by Parnell Smith

I remember it was Sunday morning. Warming up for the big game is what I was trying to do. I yawned, stretched, arched my back and almost lost my balance.

Basketball and almost 60 years old is like mixing peanut butter with pepperoni pizza. Have I lost my mind? But this should be fun, it's the 50 and over fellows.

Let's put the "ny" on the end of "fun" when all of us have bad knees, broke backs, and crooked necks, not to mention ankle problems and gout. (WOW!)

We're on the court and it smells like a Mentholatum room, they have some real fancy wraps and bands (orthopedic of course). No one is hyping the game, the grunts are loud, it's tense, for no one can do a full squat or a body twist.

The whistle blows to start the game, ref tosses the ball and the players reach for it; they don't jump, just reach.

Thinking to myself "50 and over"? This shit should be called "Basketball-Over!"

We still have the memory, but the bodies have long retired. One day we'll get that in our minds.

It's on. Dribbling, yeah, and slobbering also. Pass the ball, OK, then pass out. Blood pressure's up. Our pressures are higher than the score 186/98. Someone screams "lay-up, lay-up!" and we did, for the next week, recuperating. We could have opened a pill mill with all the Motrin and Ibuprofen we had.

The fast break was the highlight. We were breaking fast as we could, called all the timeouts in the first quarter, not for strategy, for breathing exercises.

50 and over. So is our game days.

Prison has done us wrong.

Merge With Me
by Wil-Lie

VERSE
There are many doors in this house
You don't even have to knock
As you wander about
You will soon find out
That you are never alone

CHORUS
There's no stairway to climb
To get to heaven
No ocean to cross to be free
All you have to do is seek the key
And then you merge with me

VERSE
Some door will open to a place
Where you are happy and free
And then comes the beast
Your heart will skip a beat
You holler and scream
And then you wake up from your dream

CHORUS
There's no stairway to climb
To get to heaven
No ocean to cross to be free
All you have to do is seek the key
And then you merge with me

VERSE
As you take a deep breath
And look within
There's a door where there is
No beginning or end
I take you somewhere
I meet you nowhere
And that is now here
And that is now here

CHORUS
There's no stairway to climb
To get to heaven
No ocean to cross to be free
All you have to do is seek the key
And then you merge with me

What Now Means to Me
by Mathew Morton

Right this very second–in this moment and as you read these words–somewhere in our world someone is going through something. Another is completing a task, while a different person has begun a new one. You are at one place and somebody else is in another. As we envelope our minds around the currently and presently, let us think to ourselves: How much weight does "now" carry?

Everything that happens in an instance becomes past, without a measurable moment going by. So what do we mean to "live in the now"? Is it a rhetorical saying meant only to keep one focused on their current objective, or is the word now used as a state of being? Can I do anything now? As I think these words, they are a futuristic glimpse of what I will type; and as they go onto this Word document they become thoughts I already had, words that already have been typed.

Now I am in prison, this much is irrefutable. However, it is outweighed by the amount of time I've been in prison, and pales in comparison to the time I have left (by what the papers say, anyway). Is now something one can try to hold onto, or cheer for–like a hero in a storybook, who is detrimentally outnumbered or outclassed? The biggest question I seem to ask myself on this topic is: does it really matter?

All life is a matter of perspective. If I think and believe "living in the now" is more important than dwelling on my past, I put less weight into it and I have a better thought pattern overall (I think most would agree). If I focus too much on my present and think not of my future, some might say that would cause a higher probability of erroneous consequences.

If I refuse to be deterred from my path by others' opinions and live my life well, without many problems, then I of course did the right thing. If I live with too many mistakes and don't take anyone's advice–and that advice, more than likely, could've possibly brought a more beneficial outcome–then I was a fool who made irreversible mistakes. But, what does that have to do with now? Nothing, it's a rhetorical question that brings me to my point.

We "live in the now," always. It is of my opinion that we cannot let hindsight rule us or bring us too much sorrow. At the same time, we can't allow our future to stall us, whether through fear or excitement. Now will mean many different things to a variety of people; it can change depending on the situation at hand.

To me–as I type this and reflect on my thoughts and beliefs– now is something we cannot ignore or get away from. It is our decisions and how we live our lives. It is not something we can dwell on, because it becomes our past.

Now, I think that I may have not typed a worthy article. But now, I cannot do anything about it, except hope. In the future it could be a stepping stone to my hobby and lifestyle as a writer; on the other hand, it could instead become something I regret in my past. As for right now, I will end this and hope for the best. I will continue with things I can currently do and projects I can continue now.

In conclusion, don't dwell on the things that take you out of a positive mindset and don't stray from things that can get you there. If, for instance, an idea or project (like defining the word now) takes too much time and gets you frustrated–to where you can't think straight–don't worry about it now. Or, if you feel that the idea or project is needed in order to become a better person, then, get it done now, while you have the time and before it's too late!

Three Short Plays
by Brendan L. Terry

One
Insani-Tea: A duet of Tea and Love with Madd Jack and his Beloved
Bree

Madd Jack: You care for a cup of tea? A cup of tea for me,
    preferably, with two cubes of sugar and a tad bit of cream for
    me. But, we have no sugar nor any cream, so a plain ol' cup
    of tea is fine for me.

Beloved Bree: Aaahh, I see you are drinking your tea, with two
    cubes of sugar and a lil' bit of cream for thee? But, we have
    no sugar and we are all out of cream, so you must enjoy your
    plain ol' cup of tea, made for thee.

Madd Jack: Ah, my love. My Joy. My heart and soul, and
    everything I can't control, she is coming to enjoy with me, a
    lovely cup of tea. Please come and sit, indeed and join my
    lovely tea party.

Beloved Bree: Yes, I am, for, I love this man. He may be mad and
    condemned, but I shall ever be with him,and as you
    obviously see, I will always join him and his lovely parties
    involving tea.

Madd Jack: Oh, no. Oh, no. I travel barefoot through the snow,
    and without a shirt, I carelessly roll through the mud and dirt.
    I feel my mind going mad, but my body going glad. Never
    angry or even sad, for what I got, or losing all I had, so I shall
    drink a cup of tea and at ease the mind of me, for what

it once was, it shall always be, my name and it remains as
Brendan Lee Terry.

Beloved Bree: Oh! Deary, deary, how frightful and eerie, they are
coming to take you away, and put you inside 'til another day.
They are almost here to put you up and take away your own
tea cup.

Madd Jack: Indeed, indeed, they are coming with greed, to take
away my cup of tea, the one that so rightfully belongs to me.
They come to take me away until the next sunshiny day, so to
you my love, and the others, I bid farewell, for they are
coming to take me back to hell, where there awaits no tea
for me. I will not fight, though I am in the right, for they have
a pointy weapon that goes inside the skin, and its purpose
will be held, to make me numb and dumb again.

(Madd Jack, after returning to his cell, turns from examining his
facial hair in the mirror and asks the guard...)

Madd Jack: Excuse me, kind sir, but I was wondering if you had a
razor, to get rid of some of this fur. I understand you can't,
but if you could I was hoping you would. If next time you
come to visit, and if you so wished it, you could get it right
out of your pocket, and stand next to me–in case the blade
gets shaky to stop it. I would thank you, oh, so much,
knowing that I'm only a clutz.

Two

Can-tea-na Day: A solo for Madd Jack to the occupants of his tea party

Madd Jack: Peach tea is horrible, but my Beloved Bree is adorable.
About her, my mind is always thinking, making this tea that
I'm drinking, taste wonderful this evening. With her, my life
has meaning. For her, I truly do care. Oh, yes, my canteen I
should share, so I run to my mirror, and lo' and behold, my
best friend is there. "Would you like a Snickers?" I ask him.
He just nods his head with his stupid grin. I go to hand him
one and the silly bastard tries to hand me one facing
backwards. I tell the mad man, "I'm not giving you a
Snickers, to receive a Snickers." Oh, boy, were we laughing.
"Why don't you eat yours and I'll eat mine," was my
suggestion, and that's what we did, all the while jestin'.

Three

Agrava-tea-ng Day: A duet about annoying roommate habits, with Madd Jack and his Beloved Bree

Madd Jack: Sipping my cup of tea, sitting on my bunk talking to my roomie, I tell him about Bree, but he doesn't want to hear me. He keeps mumbling of how fire will set one free. He keeps talking loudly.

Beloved Bee: Have you tried asking him to listen, and not talking about us kissin'? Maybe the fire is what he is missin'. Did your tea have all the fixins?

Madd Jack: Just two Equals. No cream or sugar, but I'll take your advice one step further. I'll tie him down and force him to hear, if I got to shout in his ear, I'll gag him if he won't be quiet. Yes, I'll teach him how to be silent. Manners, manners, is what I say. Perhaps, manners I'll make him learn this very day.

Beloved Bree: How'd you get tea in your cell? I thought they said it didn't mix with you well. And, two Equals, to boot. Just how good did you kiss that foot? Too much and too far. You take it to the dark. Why treat your roomie so? You haven't given him enough chance to grow. I think I would know. You're just setting yourself up like a pro, but you will fall flat on your face, worsen your case, lengthen your stay, and all in the course of this very day.

Madd Jack: My Beloved Bree is wise indeed. I licked no toes for my need. Just pocketed my greed. They don't always search me, and on occasion, I get my inside tea. Somehow, I should make him pay. He talks of nothing but fire, every day. Makes me want hot tea right away, but I cannot, to my dismay.

Beloved Bree: Well, the time for your party is coming to an end. As always, you leave me with a grin. I hope don't do nothing grim. Remember not to sin. Listen to your heart from within. A pleasure today, as always, it has been. One last question, I'll put it simply: isn't your cell always empty? I thought you had a one-man cell. Did they move you because you're doing so well?

Madd Jack: Not quite. I'm still by myself to keep from a fight, but the bugger in there is crazy, I swear, he's always staring at me through the mirror, and when a guard comes, he always vanishes into thin air. One last cup of tea, then it's back to my padded room for me!

Sheets Wappering in the Wind
by Rudy Vandenborre

Lingering in front of the cell window. Mostly to cool off by that trickle of air flowing through the small holes in the metal window cover. The top part has that opaque plexiglass...a room with no view.

Still, he remained there. Staring into the past...a time almost forgotten. Reminiscing about that young, happy teenager, often confused, desperate and very lonely.

The boy, born in Belgium, a European country.

Raised by a doting grandmother.

A small farmer's town...the nearest city 15 miles as the crow flies, however, city life and the town's happy atmosphere so much different...another century apart. The town had in the sixties - seventies 2 railroad tracks but no train station, no square large enough to hold weekly markets, kids but no school, youngsters went to the nun's kindergarten school, lots of public drunkenness but no police station, not even a shopping center...heck it did not even have a traffic light.

However, you saw miles and miles of farmland, green pastures where the cows lazily grazed, horses had plenty of space to run, small patches of forests where youth built their clubhouses; inside those experimenting with the many "firsts."

A town where people greeted each other by their name. Now in today's society a new car in the driveway signifying a measurement of wealth...then, most houses didn't even have a driveway let alone a car.

A town where front doors didn't need a lock, the backdoor stood always open, some houses built new, others from around the turn of the century. The boy and his grandmother lived in such an older house...small, cozy, warm, their home. Still had an outhouse. In the summertime to be shared with flies, spiders and other insects;

in the winter you froze your butt. When the boy moved to the city at the age of ten, he saw his first bathroom complete with a bath and shower; before that discovery he took a bath in a large laundry tub that grandma filled with hot water.

When the pastor shouted the last "amen" of the evening and with his flock trampling down the aisles indicating the end of the service, the cafes around the old St. Katherina church became small goldmines on Saturday evening. It was no unusual sight to even see the priest with a monk's brewed Trappist in his hand.

School's summer break lasted all of July and August...for a farmer these months signified hectic times, long days with hard work, the crops in the fields needed harvesting and brought into the barns. The boy, eager to help out, reaping potatoes and cucumbers on his grandmother's farmland...and even offering a helping hand to the other farmers.

One late August evening, with the day's labor in the bag, the farmer invited everybody to a sampling of some homemade cider. In the coolness of the indoors, the boy guzzled more than his share of the sweet but very potent apple juice turned cider. Even now, after all these years, how he made it back home remains one of his unsolved mysteries. What he does recall...that grandma gave him a plastic bucket before he laid down in bed.

His last thoughts of the night: why did she give me this bucket?

The next morning, the neighborhood saw the aftermath of the boy's cider drinking, as in front of the house, hung on the clothesline…sheets wappering in the wind.

A New Day
by Roderick Mathis

Fear is a part of my every wakeful hour. Being inside these fences of the wakeful, I mean walking dead for twenty-seven years, nine months, and four days is a determining factor. At times it feels as though it generates from doubts of never being physically free; "Is this my end?"

Sometimes it appears that I've been in this endless landscape of a world all my life. "When is it going to end?"

Never-ending seas, no land in sight; I'm a piece of driftwood floating on ocean waves; a storm brewing, dark clouds rolling in, no sunshine to be seen; where is the man that walks on water when I need him most?

Oh, my God, please have mercy!

He hears my plea, it seems at times because the storm abates and sunshine and warmth enter my being for just a moment and everything is bearable in this landscape of the wakeful dead.

Sleep comes and goes when I arise into a new day. "Fear is on the scene once more…"

Pedagogy of a Dutch Neger
by Giovanni O. Sairras

The cold and dense beads of sweat gently rolled down my
warm adolescent cheeks
like silent tears bled from mahogany-colored eyes
                    my members
                            frozen stiff
from fear that gnawed at my knees and ankles
like invisible rodents
                    as I stood there
                            motionless
                                    blank faced
she hurled a barrage of racial epithets toward my expressionless
facade
                    unexpectedly
proceeded the dark expressions that crushed the impressionable soul

        "Negers heben geen hersen."
She chanted her favorite mantra in a stern Dutch accent
My countenance fell
                    as her cadence rose
plateauing at an ominous tone
she reiterated carefully
                    every line
                            every syllable
carefully accentuating her scorn for her swarthy student

        "Negers heben geen hersen,"
The words sprang forth from the tip of her thinly crafted
                    slits
                            for lips
as she mechanically paced to and fro across a cramped
enclosure of a classroom.

Though at seven I knew she was implying the so-called
        curse
placed upon the "Niggers with no brains," by the very same
God they so deeply venerated
Our intellectual inferiority,
        she began,
was the result of a genetic deficiency relegating us to the
unfortunate fate of a life of servility to her pale-skinned
ancestors who were undoubtedly created in the image and
likeness of God,
        she attempted to explain
                to my young mind.

As the unfortunate offspring of a Christianized third-world
democracy,
                we've all been afflicted
                        by the myth of black
                                inferiority.
Its presence permeated our wretched existence:
                during the fiery Sunday sermons,
                        over the solemn prayers
                                at mealtime,
even across the steep hills and valleys tapering into the
        dense jungle
of our small Dutch republic where disgraced Maroon settlements
                clustered together
                        like constellations.

Here, those pernicious fables of black inferiority reverberated across
the arborous landscape like the
                thunder
                        of a thousand
                                roaring
drums bellowing the silent cries of scornful souls as they

feverishly danced away their bitter pain over the angry
   flames
     of a midnight
      bonfire.

Ironically, we were well-acquainted with these European fairy tales
way before we were old enough to articulate our first words.

And so our psychological conditioning abounded.

Four and a half centuries it resounded
echoing across the remote vestiges of time and space
until it had finally returned where it had once began—
    the New World—
the land where the fair-skinned gods had anchored their
    great
      war ships of wood and metal.

"O how the 'negers' had disgraced the love of the Most High,"
she sang in an ominous voice
    while clasping her arms
      together in a tight
       embrace
as she gazed into empty space as if staring at a ghostly apparition of
some invisible deity spectered across
the classroom—
     nodding an assuring smile of approval.
"Their benighted skin—the curse of a sinful race,"
    she snickered menacingly
      like the sinister chuckle of a stepchild.

I became a casualty of her inborne prejudice
before she would end her distasteful symphony of
racial inferiority

Martyred by her ignorance
            psychologically devitalized
and forever scarred by words that seemed to express
an abiding truth transcending generations of
Surinamese creoles

Across the African diaspora
these mournful songs were sung.

Now!!!
by Ollie Edward Parker III

Every day is a struggle.
I live in a world of chaos and violence.
I never asked for this, yet I chose this life.
Having no guidance, no direction or purpose.
As I sought to conquer this insanity that
devoured my purpose unjustifiably. Unanswered questions riddled
my life before
I became a teen.
Anger dominated my rationality, and pulverized
my morality to the point that I shunned
discipline and principles. Who can say what I could have become?
What I could or should have done? I can only say the past is the past
and the future is tomorrow…And today right now is the present.
The presence of my turmoil is like a cancer that is slowly chipping
away at my soul. Beating me into a corner, like a boxer
in a title fight hanging on the ropes being pounded by a no-named
opponent.
As flashes of past defeats project off
his mind. He refuses the agony of being defeated.
Rallying the last of his strength in the final seconds of the last round.
To administer a knockout. Society looks at me as if I were a plague.
Judged on fear, ignorance, deceit, racism and bigotry. Prosecuted
through perjury. Justice or just us the past never died and if you
think there's been a change, your perception's a lie.
For the past is the past…
The future is tomorrow…
And the present is now!!!
Again I never asked for this, yet I'm here in a world of chaos and
violence. Sometimes I feel like there's no room 4 love
in here or in me

cause a lot of people say that they love me,
yet their actions show me different. No one knows the pain I hold so deep inside. No one knows the reason y these scars decorate my arms and soul!!! Nor is it for them to know...I realize that my mistakes, my failures have had far-reaching effects. That I was once a selfish individual, once upon a time.

I don't know what the future may hold. I don't know what tomorrow may really unfold. But I do know that I can't change the past. I can only build a better future. And learn from my mistakes. NOW!!!

Un-used Labels
by Gerald "Broken" Pool

Now, oftentimes when an individual hears the title of inmate or prisoner, a positive connotation does not come to mind. Being a prisoner myself, I view those words as stigmas. Many labels have been carved upon me over the years of my incarceration. Labels such as Inmate, Prisoner, Convict, Convicted Felon, just to name a few.

Subsequently, I evaluatively and introspectively question myself…with those imposed labels, does society even consider other labels for me? To wit: Father, Husband, Brother, Friend, Mentor, or maybe even Author. Society's descriptive labeling of an individual is how one's self worth is defined, especially when letters of the alphabet follow your last name such as A.A., B.A., P.H.D., R.N., L.P.N., M.D., ESQ. Just to name a few, and I can't help but wonder, have those diligently earned alphabetically titled individuals ever taken into consideration that a great number of the incarcerated also shamefully wear the label of "victim" from the circumstances and experiences endured while doing their time and humbly paying their debt?

As labels given by society's standards are the norm and tell the worth of an individual, they never tell the story of survival or redemption for those who have been labeled incorrigible, damned, or a "dead man walking." So the next time you hear someone pass judgement on someone who is incarcerated, please, for them, for me, try and remember that despite our poor decision-making skills, crimes, or wrongs to society, we are, in fact, still human beings, we are still people with thoughts, aspirations, goals, and emotions. And, many of us have dealt with pains and sorrows that have scarred our innermost souls.

In the incarcerated realm, the Battle Scars that you physically wear make you a warrior in the "land of the gladiators." But, the biased, judgmentally viewed labels given by the unknowing never truly define who or what we are, nor the ability of what we can potentially become, not in a distant future that is already overfilled with heartaches, good intentions, and counterfeit promises, but now.

A Line in The Sand
by Israel Martinez

I got beat up by a two-year old; I was one.

Being a one-year old and getting creamed was life-changing. I never heard of someone getting whooped at that age. The bully's name was Frederico Noa. He was later nicknamed Red Fred–this was because in all of his fights he drew blood. I was the first one.

The details of that event are fuzzy. I mean c'mon, how much can a one-year old really remember? What I was able to recall was that I lost, and my bloody nose was the reminder.

My father filled me in on the details as I got older. It seemed like it was all he could remember of his son. "Boy, your ass got smashed. You can't be mah seed 'cause you took dat hit as well as a cat gettin' wet." My role-model.

I mean seriously, how am I supposed to look up to this jackass I have dubbed "Sir?" The former fits better but I would have got whooped for calling him that.

My loving mother, God bless her soul, was day compared to Sir's night. "My poor baby, I remember that dreadful day. That Noa child was a monster. Your beautiful blond hair was all mussed up and your sweet face was covered in dirt and blood." My protector.

She passed away shortly after those words. I was only six at the time. Sir brought me up, which made things even more difficult. You see, Sir liked to drink and loved to gamble. The only activity he enjoyed more was beating my ass silly.

"This will build character," he would say, right before slapping me dead across the face. "My son will be no pussy and he sure as hell better not lose another fight." The next blow was usually a backhand on the other cheek.

It seemed my father took the loss of my first fight as a personal affront to his manhood. It didn't matter. He wasn't much of a man anyway.

Getting beat every day did some good for me, especially when Sir got creative and hit me with any loose object in the house. The beatings made me tolerant to pain. I picked fights with the school's bullies in elementary and beat the snot out of 'em.

Unfortunately, Sir did not like that either. "My son ain't gonna be no 'linquent. You fight; you do it without gettin' caught." And then the belt buckle would smash across my back. Those kind of blows built the most character.

I didn't see Red Fred again until high school. By then, he had become an accomplished bully. He seemed to enjoy fighting almost as much as I did.

"Null, there's a dude named Fredericio Noa at our school." David was the first to call me Null. It was a play on my first name, Nollie. "He goes by a wicked name with a bad rep and he is callin' out anyone who wants to square up with him. He's trying to claim pissin' rights to the school."

That was David. He was a good friend. Loyal to a fault, but he was always at my fights.

I had significantly fleshed out from our first fight 14 years earlier. My genes were good to me. Thanks, Sir. I ended up being six feet and change, 190 pounds, long blonde hair still. I looked forward to my rematch.

My then girlfriend, Alexandra, did not like me fighting. But David and I went to meet up with Red Fred anyway, to decide on when and where.

Fred had not improved over the years; his forehead pushed far off his face and the look made him a close cousin to a caveman. Shocks of fire hair covered his scalp. Maybe the name really came from his hair. I didn't put much thought to it because I was flared up for round two.

Red Fred looked me up and down. It looked like it took him a few moments before his mental synapses fired and made the connection.

"Whelp, whelp, whelp. Nollie, how's your nose?" Very funny guy this one. "I really hope you're ready for another ass-whupin'."

We decided to meet up behind the portables during lunch. All the kids would be in the cafeteria and that would leave us free to our fight. The only ones present were Red Fred, David, and me.

"So, you need a little whore to help you fight, Nollie? Figures after the whupin' I gave ya."

"Noa! There's no reason for you to attack Dave. He was there when we decided on the fight so lay off. He just wants to enjoy the show."

Fred looked at me as if I had a screw loose. "Whatever you call your little whore is on you. Let me reintroduce you to my fi---."

Well, I am not ashamed to say that I did not let him go on. The resounding crack of my fist connecting to his face thrilled me. The look of hurt on David's made me act insane. Before I understood the extent of my attack, I had Fred on the ground and was pummeling his face with bloodied fists.

The sound of a girl screaming broke my focus. I looked up to see people staring at me. The police arrived after the ambulance. David tried to get me up to run but all I could do was stare at Fred's caved-in face. When the paramedics removed the body, a howl escaped my lips. I felt all the pain in my gut and it forced the sound out; bystanders gave me a wide space.

David and Alexandra watched as they handcuffed me. Alex came to my side in tears to kiss my cheek. When they pulled her away I could hear her sobs as they put me in the back of the police car.

I was charged with involuntary manslaughter but given a youth offender sentence. Imagine Sir when he came to court and heard the charge. I smiled the whole time I was there. When they came to remove me, I gave Sir a parting shot. "I got caught. I guess being a delinquent was in the deck for me."

Sir's face went a deep red color before he turned and left the courtroom. They gave me a sentence of six years plus four on probation.

I was released from juvenile detention after four years, good behavior and all that. I was not a good boy though. I smoked, drank, and fought almost every day. The corrections officers were just never able to catch me and the ones who did were dirty and usually supplied the stuff I needed or bet on my fights.

Now 19 and free, I went to the only place possible for me to live. Sir was thrilled. The head doctors didn't see him as a problem. I was the problem, apparently. I just didn't fit the bill of an abused child. More like a disturbed one.

"Welcome back, ya lil' shit! Ya thought you was funny at court, huh?" And now the classic slap to the face. "The police questioned me and so did them doctors of yours. How dare you tell 'em about what you deserved!"

I held up a hand as if requesting a time-out to stop his assault.

"Well, what do ya have to go do, tinkle before the ass-whupin' I'ma give ya, I bet your behind got turned out in prison and you tinkle sittin' down like a lil' bitch!"

Crack. The hammer in my other hand hidden up my shirt sleeve made sure he could not get off another sentence. I guess Sir never figured I would retaliate. All those years and I took all the pain. I mashed in his brain. There was no way I was going to allow him to live another day.

I called the police and told them of my father's demise. They asked me who did it. I still had the hammer in my hand. Blood and brain matter dripped from my fingers.

"Whelp, that pretty much sums up why I am here, talkin' to you. Now Doctor Klein, what is your diagnosis?"

The Luncheon
by David Subil

I've seen him over the years, in the pill line waiting to get his medication. An old man with secrets to tell. Maneuvering in a sea of blue uniforms bypassing the chow line, his walker, three-wheeled for agility, weaves to the front of the line to cut in front of me. I'll let him in, he's an exception. Old is one. Canes, casts, and walkers round out the list. Three times a day men choose between basic human courtesy and not looking soft. It takes years to deprogram what your mother taught you about humanity.

Food trays shoot out of the small concrete window, bright red fluorescent cup on the tray. Salt and pepper crap shoot. "I got you Pop," I tell him, grabbing his tray and mine. They're greasy from the quick wipe down the Cons give them after every use. He's already down the aisle headed towards the handicapped tables. They're just like the other tables except instead of four rusted steel octagon seats they only have two.

Turning his walker around he sits on its cracked cushion seat. I sit next to him on the cold steel. The shit eaters don't fuck with you when you're at these tables. If you can score one, take it. Everyone else gets two minutes to eat, "Row 1 you're walking and eating," I hear, "row two you next." We're safe here. They never get this far.

The prison I.D. clipped to his shirt is faded. Kafka it reads. His prison number starts with zero, old school, been down a while. The picture on the I.D. not of the man I share a table with. Pictured: a fighter, square-jawed and mean looking. Takes no shit. Gives you plenty even when you don't order any. The man next to me, frail and spent, crooked fingers, coughing, yellowish, bald.

Over the noise, I yell "How you been Pop?"

"I'm good," he says. "Haven't seen you at Friday services anymore," he tells me. His voice, low and scratchy from years of smoking, rips down to the fingertips. "I'm not a people person Pop, if it was just you and a couple of the other guys I'd go, but fuckin hypocrites there, don't want to be around them." I tell him.

Yakisobi today. Cold noodles & cabbage, uncooked carrot coins, watery mushy zucchini. One of the better meals. Hard to eat with a spork, just shovel the food in, table manners forgotten.

"You go for you, not for anyone else," he tells me.

"I know, I'm just not a congregator. I have a problem with people," I tell him. Silent disappointment his response. "You're a good Jew, Pop, I really appreciate it, don't think I don't, and if you have to tell me every time you see, me go ahead, I won't get mad. I promise I won't. In fact, it makes me feel good," I tell him.

"So come," he tells me.

"You know Pop, I'd love to be drinking champagne right now, maybe by the pool at the Ritz, looking out at the ocean, watching the cruise ships head out. Champagne, Pop, the nectar of G-ds, the meaning of life," I tell him.

"I wrote something on the meaning of life once," he tells me.

"No shit," I say. "I'd really like to hear that one day," I say.

"Come this Friday and I'll tell you about it," he says.

I pick up his cup, put it in one of the empty squares on his tray. "C'mon, Pop. I'll walk you back to the dorm."

For You
by Michael Gonzalez

There are 171,476 or so words in the English language,
around 150,000 in the Spanish tongue,
but I'm struggling to find one
that could adequately express my anguish
at the fact that right now
I can only hug you with my eyes.

Like the most beautiful sunrises permanently etch themselves
on your mind,
there was no resisting your light insinuating itself
in mine.
Your presence in my life is laundry just removed from the dryer.
Your "I love you"s are butter pecan ice cream on my tongue.

I was scared breathless to think that I was placing a piece of myself
in the most precarious of places--
someone else's heart.

The experience...bitter/sweet,
but in a good way--
like some candy is.
and, frankly, it's...
an experience I never felt I'd deserve.
But now I yearn
for your arms around me
because you never doubt that I'm better
than the worst thing I ever did.

When storms lurk on the horizon of your eyes,
others can cower.

But I'll be here with you.
And for you.
Because you've weathered mine.

Statue of Liberty
by Juan Leal Esquivel

Statue of Liberty, you're not for me. You see, between the 1890's and 1920's millions of European immigrants passed by you as they entered the United States though Ellis Island.

Emma Lazarus wrote a poem about you calling you a mighty woman whose torch and flame are the imprisoned lightning, and Mother of Exiles. That from your beacon hand glows worldwide welcome, and that you lift your lamp beside the golden door.

But I ask myself, what would Emma write today? And would your sculptor Frederic Bartholdi still include your seven spikes to symbolize freedom's light shining on the seven continents and seven seas?

Would he still make you 151-feet tall? Given the fact that President Trump has made you seem so small! Would he still call you Liberty enlightening the world? Since that is not so, especially not to Mexico. You see, this President wants to replace the golden door with a border wall, and the Dreamers? His motto is, deport them all!

These young immigrants brought to this land, yearning to be free from the tyranny, poverty and misery. For them, there was no golden door, no beacon to guide them ashore. It is said that your stature, face, and attire come from the Roman goddess Libertas, who represents freedom from tyranny and oppression, which is what the broken shackle at your feet is supposed to indicate.

But, I ask myself: did Bartholdi know that slave ships came to your shore? Where were you during Jim Crow? "Lady Liberty," what hypocrisy, a fallacy! This is not the land of the free where millions of us fill the penitentiary.

You represent a nation that profits from these modern day plantations, and the White House? Is a mad house! Where your

President tweets all day calling Haiti and Africa shithole countries, while requesting more immigrants from Norway?
What more can I say? Do my words matter anyways? Do Black Lives matter to you?

Do you hear the screams of those young immigrants with dreams? Did you hear those children crying for their momma as they were getting beat down in Selma, Alabama? Are you aware? Do you even care? About the current state of our affairs? Where your President's obsession is to continue the oppression, creating confusion to evade his Russian collusion! "Fake News!" He spews.

But, by trying to justify his alternative facts existence, he fuels the Resistance! And so, we must unite! Fight for our plight! Some of us shall write, the Truth Teller shall rise! Exposing the lies, like the tablet of Law that you hold in your hand commemorating in Roman numerals, the "Independence of this Land." What a sham! But, what do you know, Lady Liberty; How does it feel to be surrounded by tyranny and slavery?

Would you even exist if the original Indian Nation would've had a system of immigration? There would've been no need for the Emancipation Proclamation or Abraham Lincoln's assassination! Would you be standing there at all if the Indians had built a border wall?

Butterfly Effect
by Gary Fields

It's been said that the flutter of a butterfly's wings on a dusty Savannah in Africa can set in motion a chain of events that can lead to a hurricane bearing down on Florida's east coast. Now, that may seem far-fetched, but let's see if we can visualize such a thing.

Let's say that a butterfly emerges from a cocoon and spreads its wings. That sudden movement could startle a bird to take flight. That bird could cause the whole flock to take off, and start a stampede of nearby zebra. The dust that rose into the air from the pounding of thousands of hooves could get caught up in a jet stream and be carried out over the Atlantic. There, high up in the atmosphere, the dust particles and water molecules could form a depression. From depression and tropical wave, to storm warning. The next thing you know, there's a hurricane taking aim at Florida's east coast. So, the next time you find yourself at Home Depot stocking up on hurricane supplies, you can blame it on those damn African butterflies.

Meteorologists might scoff at the simplicity of that analogy, and scientists have some pretty fancy terms for this effect: a chaos theory, cascade effect, or deterministic chaos. But no matter what we decide to call it, we can see evidence of the butterfly effect all around us. We can see it in scripture (where some might call it "the hand of God"). We can see it in nature and among nations. We can see it played out in society, in our communities, and in our personal lives.

Ever since man's original fall from Grace in the Garden, we've been looking for something, or someone to blame when things go wrong. Adam claimed, "It was the woman that you gave to be with me, she gave me of the fruit and I did eat of it." In one smooth move, Adam managed to blame both God and the woman. And Eve? She said, "It was the serpent. He tricked me and I did eat." So now, most of us can blame original sin on Adam and Eve, and it was they who set in motion a chain of events that, perhaps, led Bruce Jenner to say, "Call me Caitlin."

The fact is, the butterfly effect has been setting things off long before Queen Latifa made that movie. But far too often, by the time we begin to notice the effect, we're in the midst of some kind of catastrophe.

Many people say that the extreme weather we see each day on Good Morning America is the result of Global Warming. That greenhouse gases and the burning of fossil fuels could be causing climate change and shifting weather patterns. Now, we might not agree on the causes, but we can clearly see the effects when wildfires are burning out of control in several western states, and homes are being swept away by floods in other parts of the country.

In 1914, a little known Duke was assassinated in Sarajevo–a place that many had never heard of, but most would agree that his death set in motion a chain of events that led to World War I. That war merely set the stage for WWII, which, by the time the smoke had cleared, left the United States and the U.S.S.R. facing off as the last remaining super powers.

When the U.S.S.R. invaded Afghanistan in 1979, our C.I.A. used to back a "tall Arab man in flowing robes." We provided him with weapons, training and intelligence. We also helped him to develop a base of operations and recruit students and Mujahedeen to overthrow the "infidel invaders." Ten years later, not only did the Russians withdraw, but the conflict likely contributed to the eventual collapse of the Soviet Union. As it turns out, the Arabic word for "the base" is al-Qaeda, the word for student is Talib, from which we get the word Taliban, and that tall Arab man in the flowing robes was Osama bin Laden.

In 1955, a seamstress and secretary for the N.A.A.C.P. would refuse to give up her seat on a bus, and a little known preacher would organize a bus boycott. So sometimes a cascade event can produce a dream, as it did in the case of Rosa Parks and Dr. King, but far too often, what we get is chaos. For example, Rodney King made a decision to hit the gas rather than get pulled over, and it wasn't long until Los Angeles went up in flames.

But readers, what I want us to consider today is this: No one wakes up one day and says, "I want to set in motion a chain of events that will lead me into the Valley of the Shadow of Death, or to a double-digit prison sentence." So why is it that so many of us have found ourselves in that valley, or with so much "time" on our hands?

If we can recognize the fact that a negative chain of events can so easily be set in motion, the opposite must also be true. Shouldn't it be possible for us to set in motion a positive chain of events? And shouldn't we make every effort to do so? The same way that it doesn't take all day to recognize sunshine, readers, it shouldn't be that hard for us to figure out when we're walking in darkness, playing in the shadows, or on the verge of setting off a negative chain of events. Like a pebble cast into a pond whose ripples reach for distant shores, your actions will possibly impact your family, the community, or society. They could have an impact on the Nation, or even touch the world.

Now, we might not be able to stop a hurricane from forming, but we can begin taking control of our lives. We can begin striving to set forth a positive flow of events into the lives of those around us, rather than leaving a trail of destruction.

We can't control our destiny. We can't control what may be happening five, ten or fifteen years from now. We can only control ourselves, and that "one act at a time." But, each act becomes a brick, and it's with those bricks that we will lay the foundation upon which our lives will either rise or fall. What we need to realize is that each act is preceded by a thought, so let us think clearly, and act wisely. After all, we have more to work with than some damn African butterflies.

Point Being
by Marcus Jones

The Eiffel Tower doesn't look as good at one p.m. as it does at one a.m.

Fireflies get swatted in annoyance at noon but gets cradled delicately in palms hours after the sun sets.

Point being, the true fruits of a person's character reaches ripe time when you're forced to see their light shine, and that's during the night time.

Darkness itself doesn't define us, it's our attitude amidst it that does.

I've been handed lemons. It ain't turn out how I thought it would either. When Life handed me lemons, I cut them up to make lemonade and lemon juice shot in my eye. Life laughed at me in ill-humor, but I laughed too in resignation. And as my spirited laugh silenced the malice in Life's laugh, I continued to try and make lemonade with one eye squinted shut.

In the daytime, when Life is great, we're all smiles and good vibes with all negativity cast aside for our shadows to hide as they trudge behind like dutiful servants.

Until the night begins…

Because where our shadows go when the day ends, and the night begins is our hearts. When Fate causes night to fall upon our life, when we get suffocated by the smoke thick darkness of circumstance, all the negativity we've kept in our shadows reaches out from our hearts, like rusty nails in cabinets, hoping to scratch the palms of any handouts that come our way.

How often in the night do people stand on a marsh like everything is mellow and allow their souls to be roasted by the fires rising from the bridges they've burned, embracing the heat of pity from the blaze and singing campfire songs with choruses like, "Nobody knows the trouble I've seen, no, no, no...?"

Self-pity is a tireless horse. The minute you swing your leg over and straddle its back the ride is more draining than the tubes morticians put in corpses to drain any signs of life inside.

I've met self-pity, this tireless horse. Instead of riding it, I slapped that horse on the ass and smiled as I watched it ride off alone into the night.

My worst days were never as bad as I thought, because I'm still here...

Nelson Mandela was sent to prison.

Malcom X was sent to prison.

Tookie Williams was put to death.

Darkness itself didn't define them; it was their attitude amidst it that did.

Point being, the true fruits of a person's character reaches ripe time when you're forced to see their light shine, and that's during the night time.

The Eiffel Tower…doesn't look as good at one p.m. as it does at one a.m.

Fireflies get swatted in annoyance at noon…but gets cradled delicately in palms hours after the sun sets.

Today (or A Transgender Type of Day)
by SLM

There's a girl in my head,
who wants to be free.
She dreams of a field of flowers.
The dream is moving toward reality,
but it's not there yet.
She takes her megaphone in hand
and connects it to a speaker
that rock stars would admire.
She steps up to the podium.
The obscenities and litanies of despair begin.
Don't you wish you looked like her?
Don't you wish you'd been born a woman?
Look at your balding pate you disgusting male.
Look at that nasty body hair.
You're a disgrace to womankind.
It continues.
I'm on the floor in a corner of my mind.
I can't move.
Blood leaks out my eyes and ears.
I just want it to end.
That's how my day starts.
Then it's the pill line
to pick up my hormones,
the glorious, life-saving blue pills.
"Hey, where's my other hormone?"
"It's on order."
"It's been on order for three months."
"We're doing the best we can."
Your best costs me my sanity.
"Hey inmate," the officer screams.

"Sir?"
"You need a haircut."
"I have a pass to grow it, Sir."
"What makes you so fucking special
that you have a pass? Tell me now!"
"I'm transgender…"
"Get the fuck out of here."
How many times am I forced to out myself today?
At the counselor's office I pull out my list.
Why are there so many issues every week?
Can you help with the missing hormone?
Can you help with the female canteen issue?
Can you help with my endocrinologist appointment?
I was supposed to have that two months ago!
You can send requests.
You can send grievances.
You can send diplomatic cables
for all the good it will do.
Give me the help I need!!
Oh God, the pervert is staring at me again.
He's a boy who calls himself a man,
who's never known a day of responsibility.
He thinks because I'm transgender I want sex with men,
and naturally that must mean I want sex with him.
Ew, gross. I hate being male, why would I want to be with one.
Get away from me, I snarl.
My sister calms me down.
"I don't like boys."
She understands.
I wish I didn't have to be at a male facility,
but they won't give me the hair removal,
or surgery,
or anything that would let me leave this
cesspool of wannabe boyfriends,

even though I'd be happy to pay for it all.
Finally, it's master roster, lights out;
I can finally go to sleep.

There's a girl in my head.

Trouble
by Roderick Richardson

"Trouble is easy to get into, but, hard as hell to get out of," my daddy would always say. I would hear those words sitting in the backseat of a Buick LeSabre, in the fourth grade. Innocent, childish thoughts of playing floating in my mind, dreaming of becoming Paul Warfield, or Lynn Swann.

He never gave a full explanation of those words, and by fifth grade, he was gone. I grew up overnight, watching my mom struggle. Disconnected lights and evictions became common. Reality erased all thoughts of being a kid.

When kids in my neighborhood played games in the park, I was at Winn-Dixie, toting groceries, and by thirteen, I was on the street corner in Liberty City selling insured weed.

I learned at a young age that if you don't pay bills, you'll be sitting in the dark, you can't take a bath, and the really bad part is sitting in the front yard of where you used to live with all of your furniture in a pile, your ex-neighbors pointing and talking about you.

Being the oldest, I learned fast how to survive. The streets became my second home, and the people I met, my extended family.

Right and wrong never mattered. Getting the bills paid, by any means necessary, became my duty and my cause.

When things went right, everyone was happy. And when it went wrong, everyone was gone.

Now, I walk with so many memories, accumulated over the passage of time, experiences good and bad, that have made me the person I've become today.

On this long journey, right and wrong sprouted and grew right before my eyes.

I've found a higher power that lifts up my spirit even though sitting in a prison cell sometimes drains my willpower. My hope keeps me going strong.

At times I look in the mirror and see the face of that small boy sitting in the backseat of a Buick, hearing the words, "trouble is easy to get into, but hard as hell to get out of."

Now I know the meaning.

Untitled
by Stanley Pettigrew

I bare scars of solitude away from all
that I love, caged like an animal.
The keepers of the habitat allow the animals to
devour one another, sometimes provoking the challenge.

Although some of the animals aren't exempt
from their natural instinct, adapting to their
environment, getting before being got.
In that, the predators prey on the feeble.

Around election time, politicians
congregate, feeding society with the red meat of promises.
How they would be more stern in keeping
them caged as opposed to other politicians.

Society blindly adheres to these tales
with thumbs up and smiles.

In those cases, some of the animals lose sight of self and life.
Yielding to the deceptions that label them.
Many mope in darkness like antelopes
thirsty around a crocodile's pit.

What is a warning before destruction?
Is it a flashback of the past, the mocking bird
mimicking my mother's rebuke? A hard head
making a soft ass and my lying down would be a bed
of stones.

Years spent roaming from habitat to habitat,

the once black locks are few in numbers,
sprinkled salt and pepper.
The focus points are now dim, and the limbs
once held up are now fragile.

Rise up, men, be accountable.
Forget all the chatter that has stigmatized you
as an animal.
Take hold of the reins of tomorrow
with a firm grip.
For God has given each an achievable
horizon, the skies are places we can soar.

Through the Rickety Door
by Gustavo Guerra

It is so ordered that the defendant, Gustavo Javier Guerra, be remanded to the custody of the Florida Department of Corrections for the duration of his natural life.

These words, often imagined, brought such a flood of emotion when finally spoken aloud, that I really felt like throwing up. A sheen of cold sweat glistened my brow. A knot of emotion tightening, tightening, tightening in my stomach until it stretched out my lungs and I could barely breathe. The noise of my surroundings was reduced to an inconsequential din. The edge of my vision darkened, until my only reality was the words and the despair they evoked.

"Fight it, damn it…Don't go down that road again." The knot unwinds a little and I take a deep breath. I have to start walking myself off the cliff. I am the only one who can.

"We are past it. We've healed." They say it's okay to talk to yourself as long as you don't answer.

Then why does it feel so damn real? I ask no one in particular.

I know I'm safe at this point. If I acknowledge the pain, then I'm in a good place. It's when I feed the fire of despair and consciously choose to embrace the darkness, embrace the pain, and embrace the fear that I walk where angels fear to tread. God does not exist in this darkness. I stand alone on the precipice, inches from sweet oblivion as Death sings her siren song, attempting to lure brave Ulysses into the sea.

I was not always this aware though. It used to be that when I was placed in a new cell I instantly began to look for structure to support an ad hoc noose:

The bare wall?

No.

Two steel bunks bolted on the opposite wall?

Too low.

A stainless steel sink/toilet, the center piece of my throne room?

Just depressing.

The window–two slots with a three-inch opening–covered by stainless mesh?

Maybe, I will have to get creative.

The light fixture?

The sprinkler?

The exhaust vent?

There are so many viable possibilities in an 8' x 10' cell.

Whenever I spoke with others it was usually drug induced. Narcotics and psychotropic medication created an alternate reality, a doppelgänger, who could navigate the hazardous waters of life in prison without the debilitating fear that coursed just beneath the surface. I experienced a form of chemical anesthesia with such surgical precision that it obliterated anything that ever brought me pain.

The drugs made sure I would not see or hear the highlight reel of my most epic mistakes playing on an endless loop in my mind. I would not lament my crime, the victim, or all the people afflicted by my actions. I would not sit in bitterness, attempting to absolve myself by heaping all of my guilt at the feet of my childhood abuser.

It was a temporary bliss; late at night, the drugs began to lose their anesthetic properties. Darkness swallowed the distractions I donned like armor. Head on pillow, eyes wide shut, I heard the words and once again, my overactive mind taking them to their logical conclusion: A very long time from now, I am going to die alone in prison having watched everyone I loved die before me.

Daily life consisted of three stages: waiting to get high, being high, and coming off the high. I was able to mask the deep-seated fear this way. But all I really accomplished was to push it further down. The more I pushed, the more it tried to resurface. It became a daily battle where the lines of demarcation changed with the tide of inebriation.

The fear morphed over the next couple of years. It mutated into anger. This I could deal with, because this was acceptable within the norms of prison society. This was an armor I could wear which kept people at bay, kept them from knowing who I was, and how truly horrified I was that I took someone's life.

All of the disconsolation, hopelessness, and desperation changed abruptly when, six years after the crime, an inmate who worked in the chapel invited me to attend a religious retreat. I accepted, and what resulted went far beyond my meager expectations of air-conditioning and some snacks. I experienced the supernatural within the decrepit walls of a prison chapel in Chipley, Florida. Yes, the supernatural. You may ask, "How do you know?" Well, I can tell you that post-Chipley, I am not the same morbid, melancholy, borderline suicidal junkie I used to be.

How does one describe an experience with the supernatural? I do not consider myself capable of, much less qualified for, such a feat. I can describe the results. I found a wellspring–freshly dug–of hope within myself. My eyes, often burdened with evaluating my surroundings for my own demise, were now opened to others hurting in a similar way. My heart, necrotic in its existence, no longer contaminates everything I touch with the stench of death, but rather, longs to bring the hope I found to others.

And the words, oh, those fateful words, agents of hopelessness and despair, no longer induce a wail of loss within my soul, for I have used those very words to erect a memorial in my heart and mind, a warming stone, if you will, of who I am without God, and the consequences of traversing the road most travelled. It serves me well.

It is now year nine, post-Chipley. I cannot tell you I am the poster boy of mental health and acclimation. I can say that by walking through a rickety chapel door, I found an answer to the fear, hopelessness, and despair that threatened to destroy me and cause even more pain to those still brave enough to love me.

My hope is beyond. My purpose is the here and now. And, in helping others, I have found myself.

Untitled
by John Barrett

Freedom, what is it? Who is it for?
I used to think it was me but I don't anymore
I thought Americans were free
But I found out that they're not
If freedom were free I'd have some
But freedom costs far more than I've got

I've heard speeches about freedom
But everything they said was wrong
I've heard people declare they're free
But then say "Well I've got to get back home"

I think only the insane are free
Imagine it if you can
The insane care for nothing
Neither woman, child or man

They care not when, if or what they eat
Even if it's their own shit
They'll beat their head against a wall
And not know how to quit
They'll hurt you or themselves equally
With absolutely no remorse
They'll take whatever is there
They'll care nothing for the source

So, stop and think it over
Think very carefully
I'll ask a simple question
Do you really want to be free?

Attempted Escape
by Eduardo Martinez

I have a graveyard in my head. Dead faces in the lobby of my mind having lively conversations. Family members, friends, travelers, and strangers knocking shots back with my conscience. Technically, I see dead people. Not the paranormal-or-zombie type, but the buried-alive-life-sentence kind. The prisoner's fate solidified by the concrete that pressures him.

The thing is, you never quite know who you'll end up burying till life throws you a shovel. I suggest you dig deep if you don't want the memory lingering around drunk in the shadows of the lobby.

It was a Tuesday. The one day out of the week I never trust. He was new to the dorm. A slightly plump, elderly white man. He didn't look threatening. A proper haircut, tweed coat, and corn pipe would have given him the look of a scholar. He could have been a daily-double away from winning jeopardy. I sized him up, and filed him into my mental rolodex.

I first peeped him from my peripheral using the pay phone next to me. As I dialed the 21 digits required to call my wife collect and waited, I did what convicts do naturally, ear-hustled.

"Right when things were bettering—no it's been over 30 years."

"Why now, why this, I can't…"

His following words slip by as my wife accepts my call. My ears closed shop and spent the 15 minutes pushing my love through a landline.

Shortly after that, the professor and I crossed paths again. I was on schedule with the monotony of my daily routine. I was sitting on my footlocker, stirring my oatmeal. Then the hollering got my attention. Not the sound, but the tone of it.

"Yo, yo, yo-yo-yo-yo! Y'all look!

I peeked out of my room. The shouts rose as guys gathered around the four showers. Four holes in concrete. No doors, tiles the tint of spoiled mayonnaise and a push button for a showerhead that has the water pressure of a newborn. So for privacy, guys find ways to hang, tie, or clip a bed sheet like a shower curtain. Creativity can be survival in prison.

The jolly old fellow chose a sheet that fell short about two feet from the floor. Whether by chance or tarot cards a prisoner walking by saw blood hitting the tile rather than water…like sour ketchup on spoiled mayonnaise.

That's when the excitement turned up. I live on the top-tier. I stepped out of my cell, walked to my right. Curiosity tugging my vision towards the shower stalls. An inmate had torn the make-believe curtain off. I saw feet. Blood. The professor. His back was slumped against a filthy wall that has seen more balls than a slave auction.

I stood above and across from him. Looking down on him like a bird. Watching clearly from my sky box seat. He slouched, more people gathered. It became a pep rally; a sing-along to a Caucasian swan song. I've witnessed murder, beatings, stabbings, and fake attempts at suicide. But the professor was all in. No punt-faking.

Blood poured thick and dark, like chocolate syrup in a Hitchcock flick. His body seemed past caution as the hollering increased. I thought of the movie "Lord of the Flies." How normal kids became savages in order to survive and not cry. I mean we just stood there, spines straight like books on a bookshelf.

Some men broke the spell and banged on the thick Plexiglas that separates us from the officer station where they lounge in A.C. and rarely take us seriously. They banged harder and harder on the glass that separates us from everything but our loneliness.

The guards came slowly, like 911 responses in poor neighborhoods. My eyes scanned him. I tried not to avert my gaze as I found the source of his self-inflicted departure, his hands working robotically, hacking away at his skin. It looked like someone was raking a fork down the middle of a freshly baked cherry pie.

I suppose there is no need for precise slices when life hands you soda can fangs you can ram into the folds of you forearm. My eyes crept slowly up his body. He was fully dressed in Class-A uniform. As if he wanted to look presentable making his cameo in the afterlife, as if heaven and hell had dress codes.

Our eyes locked in, round and wide as handcuffs. I think he was expecting my stare. We caught eyes the way you catch someone cheating in a card game. Mouth closed, secret shared 'cause you still let it unfold and play out. I almost thought he'd wink at me, like this was all a game. But we just stared at each other.

He wore a rosary. It was smeared with blood. I didn't think sacrilegious; I thought of God. I wanted to ask him what happened and what was happening to us. Our eyes wrestled. The chants continued. The noise, the walls. His essence going down a shower drain towards freedom. Or another holding cell in hell.

The guards came. Two of them. Guys yelled, waving the sergeant down, hurrying her. Shouting, "Look-look-look-look-look."

Her first words when she reached the shower:

"Oh my God."

I wanted to tell her God isn't here right now. I don't know if it was the officer's presence or not, but the professor began to hack furiously at his forearm. Our eyes still linked. She screamed commands, "Inmate stop! I said stop!"

She clutched her pepper spray. He raked harder. She pleaded for him to stop. He bled stronger. She begged him to stop. He finally did.

The other guard's radio coughed up words of static as medical took its time like release dates. Two inmates had stomach enough to drag him out of the shower. That's when our eyes finally unlocked and lost contact with each other.

The professor lay on his back. His arm looked like a casserole. We all stared, no longer hollering. One guy took his shirt off and gave it to an officer who had enough sense to tie it tightly around the professor's arm.

We waited quietly, and watched the new guy begin to ripen, or rot. Medical eventually arrived, put him on a stretcher, and wheeled him out the dorm. The show was over; a few guys made it their responsibility to clean up everything so they wouldn't lock us down. I went back to my cell, grabbed my bowl of dense oatmeal. I spit out the first spoon, it tasted fleshy. I dumped the rest of it down the toilet. It reminded me of the old man's skin.

That same night, dozing off, I kept catching the professor peeking into my mental lobby, disturbing my conscious. The next day, the professor returned alive, walked right in through the same door we assumed he left dead through. If it weren't for the fat stitches that raced across his forearm like angry centipedes, I'd question my sanity.

I couldn't believe he was alive. But there he stood. I couldn't believe he was back in general population with no supervision, but there he was.

Ear-hustling, I heard a guy ask the professor if he was alright. Without hesitation he replied, "No."

The prisoner fired back in response, "I'ma pray for you."

I saw the old man cut his eyes like he cut his vein and said, "No. I just have to do better next time."

He turned his back and walked away, just like hope did.

Later on that evening the guards came and got him. I haven't seen him since... Sometimes, goodbyes come before hellos. I don't look at the shower floor the same anymore. It's stained with pieces of all of us scaling the filthy walls. And I'm not sure if someone, somewhere out there, is praying for us... or should we just do better next time.

Reflections
by David Hackett

Reflections of the ancient past.
A happy, out-going young lad.
Full of dreams and plans.
Then dreams were exchanged with the darker side of grace by a
terrorist blast.
The destruction of life in innumerable shards of glass.
Shattered reflections of what I am: angry, sad, introverted, self-
destructive, on alert, code red, let no one pass, not understanding,
never a laugh.

Reflections in smoky glass, unfocused shadows a primrose path.
Reflections in bubbled glass, glimpses of a brighter path.
Giving forgiveness to whoever took that life from me.

I will own the past, then let it go.
Developing empathy, and even learning to laugh.
And, when the time is right, a reflection of a second chance will be
in a refurbished piece of glass.

My First Time
by Peter Collier

Fourth grade's grimy details I need not disclose.
Nightmares haunt the childhood me.
I raise my hand to be excused,
no #1s or #2s,

But I learned the pee-pee dance by default, an escape route through
time-traveling demons.

PTSD preludes an afterthought. . .
Today I'd rather have my pills with juice but dry mouth is the way to
go when looking back.
Every time someone mentions that kid show,
The Magic School bus-
The veins in my forehead multiply,
A new science experiment unfolds.

"Don't tell anyone," he said forcefully.
"I know ways to make you pay,
You don't want to suffer do you?
Your grades to slip?
An accident to happen?"

That shaggy carpet,
orange like a Flintstones push-pop was
paint-rolled corner to corner.
I can still smell the shame that fell between.

Those rough fibers-
Scraped by knees physically, and mentally left me

with that blue handicap sign around my necklace for the rest of who knew when.

The doctors "say" I'm better now-
My classmates are all grown but I can still never recall any of their childish faces at the after-school program.

"Oh yeah, that's right"-

I was the after-school program.

Back in the hallway amongst the empty lockers filled with book bags and teachers' pet apple cores, I'd take my time, inching my way back, then slip into my own restraints, and smell the rotting fruit.

I never did understand that concept, all the kids I knew liked junk food anyway,
Ice cream could only shut me up for so long.
Didn't he realize next year we would all take sex ed classes?

Pork's Revenge
by Leroy Maybin

There are many ways to die. I would never have guessed pulled pork could be fatal. I have heard many times how dangerous swine can be and I laughed it off because of my love for bacon, until it almost killed me.

The millennium came with a flurry of new construction. Orlando Regional Medical Center ventured into research, adding M.D. Anderson's Cancer Institute. As an electrician, I loved the job. It was smart, technical, and on the cutting edge of all medical advancements. I worked alongside doctors, nurses, and even medevac pilots. But for me, best of all, there was the cafeteria that served world-class cuisine. Pulled pork cooked to perfection!

And then three months into the project, administration said, "No longer are construction workers from this site allowed to dine in the hospital cafeteria."

I was bummed. What started out as a couple of electricians catching employee discounts in air-conditioning had morphed into a perpetual muddy path from worksite to cafeteria. Talk about beaten paths! We created our own Oregon Trail, only westward expansion did not make it past the food line!

I have a fundamental flaw: I do not like to hear the word no. Maybe I have abandonment issues from being placed in behavior centers for fighting too much as a youth, or fear of rejection from being turned down by some preteen girl in grade school. I honestly do not know. I remember asking my mother for a neon yellow highlighter one day while shopping. Too quickly killing my hope with a "you know better than to ask" look, I stole the highlighter and ended up getting caught with it later.

At the hospital, I was offered extra work installing a vacuum system that would shuttle specimen more efficiently. The first phase began in ICU. We were briefed by a doctor vehemently explaining that power could not be interrupted lest life-supporting equipment sustaining critical patients would die. Realization dawned. Life's balance was truly in my hands. I was a capable and talented man doing important work.

I suppose I also struggle with entitlement issues, especially after working on critical energized circuitry after hours and on weekends. I felt cheated after being told that my lowly construction career exempted me from dining among the general public and other hospital workers. I became, in my mind, a second-class citizen, an outlying physical laborer at the low end of the socio-economic hierarchy. Just like my childhood thievery, I rebelled. I had to break free from the box created in my mind after my self-worth and esteem had been tested.

Mad, tired, and hungry is not the time for me to make the best decisions. With a head full of steam and the pride of determination, I entered the 5th floor elevator and descended to the ground level. My purpose was singular. I was going to eat in the hospital cafeteria, consequences be damned.

I could smell whatever was being cooked. Like a fish following a chum trail, my senses led the way. On the menu: Pulled Pork! Big juicy shreds of meat, cooked in a broth of carrots, celery, and potatoes, making the brown gravy that makes my heart weak for seconds. Just looking at the fare made me all fuzzy inside. I still could not believe that commercial food could look, smell, taste, and be prepared just like my mother cooked.

I thanked my good graces that the lounge area was practically empty. I was not supposed to be here, but with a meal befitting a king for under $4.00, I knew I was getting the sweetest deal in town. After working the long, hard hours, I was famished.

The food was delicious. But, no sooner than I began eating, I ran into trouble. I had taken a bite of the pork and swallowed, but I could not get the piece to go down. The sinew connected the meat into one long, stringy piece.

My first reaction was not to panic. I calmly tried to swallow...again and again. No dice. I grabbed my drink, thinking, maybe I can just wash it down, only to have water run back out of my mouth and dribble down my shirt. Realization dawned! I AM CHOKING...IN THIS DAMN HOSPITAL CAFETERIA I'M NOT SUPPOSED TO BE EATING IN!

I tried my best attempt at an incognito Heimlich maneuver, pounding my chest while beginning to gasp for a fresh breath. My building panic started to be noticed, my cover blown.

"He's choking!" screamed a terrified white lady, sounding the alarm.

With one last hope, with a closed fist, I hit myself in the chest, harder than one should ever have to hit himself. There was no way I would get caught disobeying a direct mandate by choking to death.

The hit rattled my entire body and up came the offending piece of pork. I sat there for a silent moment, deeply breathing precious air.

I looked up and saw all eyes were staring at me.

"What happened?" echoed many whispers and pointing fingers. I was too shaken to care, looking down at my plate with no care for the appetite I had a minute before.

Overwhelmed, I sat there and started to cry. How could I be so stupid? I never get away with anything I should not be doing. How many times will I go through unnecessary situations and suffer the consequence?

Sitting in that blessed cafeteria put a few things in perspective. I felt entitled, and wanting to be recognized and respected were not, per se, wrong. How I acted upon those feelings was. I could have gone to any of the doctors I worked with and asked for permission to dine when I worked after hours in the main hospital away from all the mud and dust.

Refusing to accept no as an answer has been a major flaw in my character that, until then, I refused to acknowledge. I also realized that what people had been telling me for years was true...pork will kill you if you give it the chance!

Down the Mineshaft
by Michael Anguille

Five years ago, I was imperiled. My thirties were a tidal wave closing in on me like I was a sleepy coastal town and I lacked all preparedness, all plans for how to handle my future. Addicted, lonely, confused, and emotionally stunted, I was sure to be fatally swept away unless some benevolent supernatural force intervened on my behalf–and the prospects for that looked bleak.

In my more lucid moments, which were really just less inebriated ones, I knew something needed to change, but hadn't a clue where to begin, what button to push, what door to open, so I could run through it as fast as possible. I had a long-time job I hated, a Grand Canyon of credit card debt from living well above my means, and had bludgeoned to death nearly every meaningful relationship I'd ever had. That I was a full-blown alcoholic didn't help. The cotton candy like cloud that fogged my judgment never seemed to lift and I staggered about from day-to-excruciating-day breathing, but never really living at all.

One night, after imbibing who knows how much who knows what, I remember lying in my bedroom watching the ceiling fan spin. Dirty clothes were strewn about and piled high in huge, festering heaps, my bed sheets were wrinkled and messy, and a giant cup sitting on my nightstand filled with hard faucet water and days' worth of congealing cigarette butts emanated carcinogenic incense that whirled about in the wind from the fan. I didn't believe in God at this point, and thought anyone who did was better off lobotomized, but as I lay on that bed, drowning in a liquor-laced, sorrow-filled pool of my own quagmire, I was willing to try anything. Even if it meant talking to him.

"Please take me away from here," I begged. "Please change things for me. Please let me start over."

Not even a month later, I was involved in the incident that landed me in prison.

It was jail at first and, despite the prayer I'd uttered a few short weeks prior, I'd have given a kidney to get out, to get back to the post cat-five hurricane disaster zone that was my existence. Sure, my car was totaled, I had nothing but a couple hundred dollars, and I was now the most infamous scoundrel this side of the Everglades. But I didn't care. I can pick myself up, I thought. I'll get back on my feet somehow. They even told me I still had my job if I got out. It was added wood to the brightly-blazing pyre that was my jail-induced, abruptly-intoxicant-deprived state of delusion—post-acute withdrawal psychosis at its finest.

In reality, I'd have gotten out, shown my face at the office once, then high-tailed it back to my working-from-home hole where I could thoroughly anesthetize myself outside the watchful eye of others (because self-mutilation's only truly pleasurable when there's no one around to rescue you from yourself). Never mind that I'd have had the added stress of trying to function with a huge trial looming. I chewed off my fingernails thinking the cops were coming when I had an overdue parking ticket. Who knows what I'd have done to myself if given the opportunity to be alone—with inebriants, of course—in that predicament? Paranoia alone had led far saner men to tragic fates; it'd have been a shit-show. And that's being generous.

Fortunately, God knew this because I never did get out. I thank him for it every day, now.

The first few months after I'd been denied any shot at bond were pretty rough. Just like the scars from cutting oneself take time to heal (if they ever do), so, too, do those inflicted by drugs and alcohol. The body goes into a more depressive state because it's missing the substances it's grown so reliant upon for sustenance and things seem to get worse before they get better. My body would go from sweating hot to shivering cold, my behavior from stoic and apathetic to meek and inconsolable. I ate only the bare minimum needed to survive because any more made me nauseous. I rarely came out of my cell from the paralyzing depression. Everyone looks like hell in jail until they get settled–which does happen, amazingly, but if I could see myself then, ghost white, malnourished, curly hair greasy and matted, I imagine I looked like an ethnic scarecrow that'd been blown over by the wind, shit and pissed on repeatedly by the family dog, then left to ferment in the elements. It was my lowest of lows.

It's cliché, I admit, but the good thing about hitting rock bottom is that there's nowhere to go but up. It took some time, but that's just what happened for me. The haze from my decade-and-a-half long bender gradually abated and the feeling of hopelessness that had tainted my life like a red tide for so long went with it. It didn't suck, either. It was a relief, like I'd been unbound from a medieval torture rack that had me stretched so taut I could do nothing but think about the pain. I dreamt about what it would feel like to be without the pressure. I was finally free and, by way of the fact that I'd have no choice but to start over when I got out, going to get the second chance I'd pleaded for so desperately months earlier.

After this breakthrough, no doubt owed to my newly acquired unpolluted state of consciousness, I thought back to the prayer I'd said on my bed that day. It made me wonder if everything that was happening wasn't just coincidence. On a hunch, though with some reluctance, I admit, I got a bible and started reading. Then I forced myself to talk to the religious volunteers at the jail, the same perpetually, almost nauseatingly happy middle-aged men who I'd have unabashedly called total fucking quacks months earlier. I asked questions, did research and ultimately arrived at the conclusion that everything I was seeing was true: none of this had happened by accident. Divine intervention had brought me to exactly this point so I could get my life together once and for all. It was then and there, in the windowless, cinder-blocked portal to redemption that is the county jail, that I vowed to use every waking moment of my incarceration to thoroughly reinvent myself, to make myself as worthy as possible for my eventual reintroduction to society.

The famous self-help quote is that "change is an inside job," which is to say that before anything on the outside can change, one must fine-tune the makings of their soul to make external change possible. I subscribed to this and started my makeover by working on my soul. What I didn't know, though, and what no self-help book will ever tell you, is just how laborious of a process internal change really is. It's like digging out a thousand splinters from a tiny wound with tweezers that are too big, despite being the smallest you can find. It's scary and demands meticulousness, as well, since it often requires travel to the deepest, darkest, intentionally hidden compartments of one's soul where it's necessary to sort through the contents selectively, expelling the waste, but salvaging whatever's still functional.

I did it, though. And for all its difficulty I ultimately found the process highly rewarding, as if I'd put the sand of my soul into a sieve and watched as the gems it once concealed glistened as they became visible. Years later, I cherish this treasure and instead of keeping it hidden, intend on making the finest jewelry from it, then wearing it day after day, stubbornly, obnoxiously, even, like the rich old lady who refuses to take off her diamonds for a sunbathing trip to the beach because she's that proud of them. Or wants to show them off. Admittedly, I'm guilty of both, though less due to boastfulness and more out of the joy I feel after having suppressed them for so long. God gave me these pieces of myself to wear proudly, to display shamelessly to the whole world, regardless of where I'm at or who's watching. For the first time ever, I fully intend on it.

The work on my exterior, when I finally got to it, was a whole different challenge. Before I was arrested, I was fat from the daily nuclear calorie bombs I consumed in liquor and had no muscle tone to speak of. Then, when I got to the county jail, I stopped eating and became really skinny, but still skinny with a lot of fat and no muscle. Picture a cheap lampshade from a discount store, its wire frame visible for all to see when you turn on the light it's supposed to cover. That was me. I was in horrendous shape. I could do maybe ten pushups, a few more sit-ups and the word cardio was anathema to me. It wasn't happening.

Five years later, I've gained 20 pounds of mostly muscle and would no longer teeter on the edge of a panic attack if asked to remove my shirt in public. I start push-up days with sets of 40 and work down, do sit-ups holding a 20-pound medicine ball for extra resistance, and have arms that can be measured in inches that number double digits. As for cardio, running in particular, it's become my favorite physical activity, a respite from the perpetual clamor of prison where I can put on my headphones and be one with my mind and body. I do some of my best thinking when I run.

Gone, too, with my years of incarceration, is the feeling I had in my former life of knowing I had things I should be doing, of wanting to do them, but not knowing where to start or even what "they" were. I know now, and write a ton.

It started with a couple hundred-page manual on the internet marketing business—the slimy amoral sub-strata of the corporate world I called my professional domain in the years before I had an inmate number. At the time, I thought I was writing it for ambitious family. But in hindsight, I think it was more therapy for me than anything else. My coughing up the last of an industry that's like cigarette smoking–it either kills you if you stick with it long enough, or leaves you choking on a thick, sludgy resin for years after you finish with it.

That project took me a year to complete. And, though my family never did anything with it (thank God), it had the side-effect of reigniting in me a passion for writing that I didn't know I had anymore. I have a degree in journalism and significant experience in the field. I just never wanted to make a career of it because I didn't particularly enjoy it. Today, I know that it wasn't the writing I didn't like as a journalist so much as the type of writing. There are some that will disagree with me, I'm sure, but I find news writing boring and restrictive. Not so with fiction writing, the manual I wrote (where I was allowed to be creative in describing my "process") or even writing essays like this one. These media allow me to spread my artistic wings, and most importantly to feel like I've expressed myself in a way that a reader may connect with on an emotional level rather than solely an informational one (as in a lot of news writing).

As careers go, how this will all play out when I see daylight again is hard to say. It's so easy–in this sheltered world I live in at the moment–to make promises to oneself that are impossible to keep when freedom finally comes knocking; and I'm abundantly aware of this. What I do know is that I feel exceptionally guilty if a day passes where I don't put a pen to paper, and this has to mean something. We shall see.

For now, it's enough for me, whether I'm in prison or not, to wake up every day knowing I have a purpose; not to mention being spiritually awakened, physically transformed and mentally resurrected. Don't get me wrong, it sucks that I had to come to prison for such changes to take place. But the truth is, as I tell my family and friends, nothing less severe would have worked for me. And for this reason alone, I'm grateful that I came here.

Yeah, I said it.

Prison saved me.

It's a good thing, too. Because who knows where I'd be if it hadn't.

One in a Million?
by Michael Annen

Six years ago, while at Polk Correctional Institution, I received a surprise letter in the mail. It was from a woman I had never heard of, from a city I'd never been to. The letter was brief. She simply asked if I would like to write and receive letters. Enclosed was a stamped envelope. Intrigued, I wrote back that very night.

Yes, I wrote, I would like to write and receive letters. It would be nice to have someone with whom I could share my hopes and dreams, my fears and concerns. However, I wrote: I'm not looking for any games. In fact, let me start by writing I don't need any money and I don't need any stamps. What I need is someone I can be real with. Maybe you're that one in a million?

I mailed the letter and returned her stamped envelope.

I received an immediate reply. She wrote, she was that one in a million! We started writing back and forth. Every morning I mailed a letter out; every night at mail call I received a letter. She claimed she was two years younger than me, 5'6", 97 pounds. 97 pounds! Really? If I turn sideways, you can't see me. I'm 6'4" and rail thin at 180 pounds. I automatically assumed she had neglected to place a one, or even a two in front of that 97. I'm figuring she's a large lady. Then, as I kept reading, I learned she had two daughters. Oh, yeah, big girl!

But I tell you what, it didn't matter. In just those few short weeks, we had shared so much through our correspondence that she went from my head to my heart. I wrote that night: This is going to sound crazy, because I've never met you, I've never talked to you, but I feel like I'm falling in love with you. P.S. can you send me a hundred! This was love! I asked for two hundred! Just kidding.

The next letter included a small portrait photograph. Long brown hair, a pearly white smile, and sparkling blue eyes. Very attractive. At least from the neck up.

I had just missed my month to add her number to my approved phone list, and she was quite adamant that I not call using a contraband phone. I simply could not wait six months to talk to her, so I wrote and asked if she would like to visit.

Sure, what do I need to do? she wrote. I mailed her a Visitation Request Form. I described the Visiting Park and suggested that when the time comes, she sit at the end of the long bench that faced the Shakedown-room door. I knew there would be a lot of people in the Visiting Park and certainly she would see me before I saw her. Everything was copasetic as we waited for the Visitation Approval Notice.

Then, terrible news. A national story broke about Notre Dame linebacker, Monté Teo. The star football player had been online, saw a pretty picture, and without meeting the woman, fell in love. But, she turned out to be a he. Monté had been catfished! I'd never heard such a thing. He was a laughing stock on sports radio, but I wasn't laughing. I went from picturing big girl to big dude. I wrote her that night: Don't bring that catfish junk to Polk C.I.

In her next letter, she told me that she had called the prison to check on the status of her visitation request. Wow, she really wanted to come visit. This should have been another warning sign. I became so nervous during mail call, shaking in my Crocs, waiting for that request approval. Of course, by Friday night, if I hadn't received it, I could rest easy over the weekend.

Then, one Saturday morning when I woke up, I noticed a piece of paper under my cell door. Late mail? I jumped off my bunk and snatched it up. Visitor approved! Oh my God! Did she know? Would she visit today? Was she here already? The paper was trembling in my hand. I was a complete wreck.

I hopped in the shower, shaved, and brushed my teeth. By 9:00 a.m. I was dressed and ready. Just in case. I could not believe how anxious I felt as I paced circles in the dorm. Eventually, I laughed at myself and calmed down. She probably doesn't even know she's been approved. Then, the dorm officer called my name: "Report to the Visiting Park."

It was a bright sunny morning as I took off for the Visiting Park. On my walk there, I was trying to psych myself up. "You got this, Big Dawg!" But who was I fooling? I was terrified. I debated if I should act like I had some cool pimp-daddy walk, or maybe a deep sexy voice. Nah, man, I was just gonna be me. She was either gonna like me for me, or she wasn't.

However, I did have a plan. As I neared the Shakedown-room, I placed an apple Jolly Rancher in my mouth. I figured the sweet aroma of candy would keep Big Girl close. The game plan was to walk up to this woman whom I had never met, had never said a word to, and kiss her right on the lips. It didn't matter if she was 397 pounds! I didn't say it was a good plan.

At Polk C.I., when you arrive at the Shakedown-room, the officer hands you the visiting paper; it has your prison I.D. photo and your visitor's picture. So, I checked her picture out. No photoshop shenanigans here. But, both pictures were small, grainy, black and white photos. I could barely recognize my own face! It was no help at all. This was going to be the biggest blind date in history.

I could hear the loud noise from the Visiting Park as the officer checked me in. On the other side of that door was my visitor. I wondered if she was as nervous as I was. The officer finished checking me in and said with a smile: "Have a nice visit." Did he know something?

I stepped out the door, looked toward the end of the bench. We locked eyes immediately–and I was horrified! Because sitting right there on the bench clutching her walker was a tiny 98-pound great, great grandmother! She wore Coke-bottle glasses that made her eyes the size of silver dollars as she undressed me right there in the Visiting Park. I'm up here, Grandma! She had on bright red lipstick, and make no mistake, her body language said it all.

"Come here Sonny boy and give Momma some sugar!"

I almost choked on that Jolly Rancher. It felt like I was in a vacuum tunnel. All the noise went silent. It was just me and sexy Grandma as my whole life flashed before me.

I prayed, "Lord, you get me out of this one, I'll owe you big time."

Just then, a sudden movement off to my right caught my attention. A lady in a sundress was standing up looking at me. She had long brown hair, a pearly white smile, and sparkling blue eyes. Whoa! This was my visitor and she was finer than advertised.

I stepped over Grandma's walker–I swear she goosed me– and I walked up to this beautiful woman, and without saying a word, I kissed her right on the lips. I really did. Then, I took her hand in mine, and I haven't let go since.

Just the beginning…

Now, the postscript: I came back that afternoon and told the fellas how, at first, I had mistakenly thought she was a 98-pound grandmother. They laughed and told me I had to share that with her. I did. She said, "I thought you turned ghost white."

We've been together over six years. During this time, dozens of people (visitors, other prisoners) have gone out of their way to say: "Excuse me, but we just have to tell you…you two are the perfect couple."

It's been a miracle for me to meet a beautiful woman and fall in love, and to know that I know, I know, she loves me!

Her story of how she "found" me is awesome, too. A miracle love story.

If I Had a Chance
by Allen King

Country girls have always appealed to me.
Mary Ann over Ginger every time.
Now, how did I ever get so crazy,
that city girl took my every dime.

If I had a chance to do it over again,
I would have never left your side.
If I had a chance, I would do it with you.

Sherry, I'm sorry I stopped calling
the very day I dropped out of high school.
I thought a man didn't need a schoolgirl.
Sure sign that I was an immature fool.

If I had a chance to do it over again,
I would have stayed in school with you.
If I had a chance, I would do it with you.

Country girls care about pleasing their man
more than dressing in all the latest styles.
As long as he's faithful she'll be alright.
When he comes home she'll keep him warm at night.

If I had a chance to do it over again,
we would be rolling in the bed together, right now.

If I had a chance, I would do it with you.

Country girls will always stand by their man,
no matter what he does for a living.
More often than not, they'll work together,
keeping those 18 wheels rolling forever.

If I had a chance to do it over again,
I would have spent my life with you.
If I had a chance, I would do it with you.

But I would have ruined your life, Sherry.
I guess God was protecting you from me.
I hope you found what you were looking for.
If not, give me a call if you are free.

If I had a chance to do it over again,
it's better you are happy without me.

Hmm...That's Weird

by Justin Slavinski

"Dude, let me tell you about this dream I had last night." That's how virtually every morning of mine started for years. If it wasn't one friend, it was another. I'm no shrink, I don't know what any of it means. For that matter, I really don't care. What do you expect of me, to tell you to lie down on the couch and tell me about your mother? Every dream is just as meaningless as the next. They're stories concocted by your subconscious.

Only thing is, my friends insist that their dreams are all fantastic. They're superheroes fighting crime; they have amazing abilities; every woman they can fantasize about suddenly appears naked before them. They start in, laying out these ridiculous narratives with unexpected twists and turns worthy of Hitchcock or his latter-day disciple Shyamalan. All I can think is: who cares? What's the point of all this? Are you sharing this for my benefit or yours? Do you want help or are you just sharing to share?

I realize some of my lack of compassion for stupid dream stories indicates my lack of empathy. I get that. Some other part is undoubtedly that I can't remember my own dreams most of the time. I am perfectly okay with that. My conscious thoughts are weird enough that I have no desire to indulge my subconscious but at the most rudimentary level. Those few dreams I am cursed to remember are so boring, pointless, and uninspired that I am forced to believe that those sharing their dreams with me must be making them up. And if they're making these dreams up, and they know how little I care about the content, why the heck are they sharing them with me to begin with?

And through all of this, sure, I'm thinking, "Who cares?" and "What's the point of all this?" But what am I saying? Nothing. I'm stuck listening, saying nothing, merely nodding along and inputting all the depth of the insight I can muster, "Hmmm, that's weird."

I went to therapy for a while. I was able to choose my therapist, pretty much at random from a list —the kind of thing health insurance allows you to do. Pick one of these, good luck! When initially searching for a shrink, I saw on the insurance website two identical Germanic names and dove a bit deeper. It turned out that the practice was a husband and wife team. I selected the woman, so I was probably channeling some kind of unspoken hope of experiencing latent Cinemax-style fantasies.

My therapist ended up looking a bit like Eddie Money—so there was one dream dashed right away. That said, she was helpful and insightful. The experience was the kind of thing that helped clean out the clutter of my brain. If you're honest with your therapist, you will receive honest insight. The beauty of talking to a shrink is that, really, you're doing a lot of the analysis yourself with the added bonus of a highly-paid professional asking you guided questions. She asked many deep, leading questions. She didn't simply say, "Hmmm, that's weird."

In between her elegant analysis and dissection of my personality, laying bare all the insecurities, pain, poorly conceived decisions, and misinterpretations in my life, I caught glimpses of her life. She'd occasionally share weird stories of other patients, the kind of stories that elicit wide-eyed shock. The sort of salacious details that make an amusing book. She related one about a boy whose mother had brought him in for analysis. The mother was concerned that her son had been doing inappropriate things with the family dog. My shrink brought the boy in, asked her guided questions and determined the boy was healthy, sane, and well adjusted–even if he was doing something questionable with the dog. She reported this back to the mother, who was appalled. My shrink doubled down, asking the mother what her problem was–provided the dog had no complaints.

All I could think to myself was, "Gee, who's more messed up here: the boy, the mom, or my shrink?" I found myself speechless; utterly, completely gobsmacked. How do I conversationally navigate out of this one? How do you even respond to that? "Hmmm...that's weird."

She told me another story. I can't remember what it's called when a shrink and his/her...shrinkee(?) form a personal connection. Freud had a word for it. Stockholm syndrome? No, that's not it. Anyhow, it was a more personal story about her life. Most of our sessions began with an update of what I had done in the past week, and then I'd delve into a deeper story or concern from my past that I felt required analysis. Occasionally she'd open with a question about some item or another. Some sort of cognitive behavioral adjustment she wanted to make.

This week, however, she opened with a story about her husband—her co-practitioner. In short, she had caught him cheating on her; not by sniffing his clothes, or checking his phone, or posting a PI to follow him around. She caught him by posing as a guy on a chat website and catfishing him. She broke into tears while relating this story. What am I supposed to do here? I'm not a touchy, feely person—I'm not about to leap up from the couch, tissues in hand, hug at the ready. I'm paralyzed. What do I say to the person who's trying to help me, when she herself needs help?

Sometimes, I wish I was a bit more of an empathetic person. To be able to comprehend why people come to me baring their souls, their subconscious, their dreams, would make my day. Until I get it, I'll continue on with what has proven an ineffective conversation ender: "Hmmm...that's weird."

WHAT WE DO

Exchange for Change provides opportunities for creative and intellectual engagement. We believe in the value of every voice, and we give our students opportunities to express themselves without fear of being stigmatized. When everyone has the ability to listen and be heard, strong and safe communities are formed.
Collaboration is our emphasis. Students on the outside anonymously partner with our students to foster empathy and create opportunities for individual and social change, allowing both sides to learn from the knowledge and experiences of their writing partners, all while realizing the value of events in their own lives.
With a pen and paper, students can become agents of change across different communities in ways they may otherwise have never encountered.

OUR MISSION

The non-profit organization Exchange for Change teaches writing in South Florida prisons and runs letter exchanges between incarcerated students and writers studying on the outside. By preparing prisoners for their re-entry into the outside community and preparing that community for their return, Exchange for Change provides vision and understanding on both sides of the fence.

STAFF

Kathie Klarreich, Executive Director
Skylar Thompson, Coordinator

For underwriting opportunities, additional copies of this journal, subscriptions, or ways to become involved, contact Exchange for Change at: info@exchange-for-change.org

Made in United States
Orlando, FL
18 July 2022

19908464R00071